What the Victorians
≈ Threw Away ≈

What the Victorians

Threw Away

Tom Licence

Oxbow Books
Oxford & Philadelphia

Published in the United Kingdom in 2015 by

OXBOW BOOKS
10 Hythe Bridge Street, Oxford OX1 2EW

and in the United States by

OXBOW BOOKS
908 Darby Road, Havertown, PA 19083

© Tom Licence 2015

Paperback Edition: ISBN 978-1-78297-875-6
Digital Edition: ISBN 978-1-78297-876-3

A CIP record for this book is available from the British Library

Printed in the United Kingdom by The Short Run Press, Exeter.

For a complete list of Oxbow titles, please contact:

United Kingdom	United States of America
Oxbow Books	Oxbow Books
Telephone (01865) 241249	Telephone (800) 791-9354
Fax (01865) 794449	Fax (610) 853-9146
Email: oxbow@oxbowbooks.com	Email: queries@casemateacademic.com
www.oxbowbooks.com	www.casemateacademic.com/oxbow

Oxbow Books is part of the Casemate group

For young Florence Acton

who took my great spade
and dug for bottles in Shropshire

⮢ Contents ⮣

☞ Preface ☜

THIS book has been nearly thirty years in the making: at any rate, the passion and adventure behind it have matured over that period. It was my parents who introduced me to the hobby of bottle digging in the 1980s, when it was a family hobby in certain parts of the country, and it was the books of Edward Fletcher, which I borrowed from the library, that fired my enthusiasm. Ivor Noel Hume's books encouraged me to find the human stories amid the flotsam of past generations, and to train my eyes to detect tiny objects such as buttons, beads, and coins, in rubbish dumps and on the foreshore. Later, training as a historian and archaeologist, I wanted to pioneer a way to research rubbish dumps as uniquely intimate deposits of information about past people's lives.

Anne and Martin urged me to action when they asked me to find the middens at Pear Tree Cottage. Their enthusiasm, not to mention their kind hospitality, rekindled my interest. Rupert Acton generously let me excavate such a site on his estate, where digging in sometimes rainy conditions was rendered far more agreeable by the mugs of hot soup, tea and scones supplied at clockwork intervals by Kylie and George and Alan and Valerie while I amended their view with my spade. Young Florence Acton was so pleased with the bottles that she grabbed that implement and dug for more. It was a highlight of the project to see her catch the same enthusiasm that caught me at her age. John and Hilary Ling, Linda Davey, Dennis Moye and many other members of the community at Bergh Apton, not to mention our UEA diggers Sophie, Michael, and Lucy, were untiring in their search for old rubbish from the schoolhouse. Ronnie and Jackie Pestell were most generous in their hospitality while Ben and I dug away their flowerbed, and Ben himself has been a great support, remarking on an occasion when I pulled a Codd bottle from the bottom of an eight-foot hole, 'I love those ones'. So did the Victorian children who broke them to recover the marbles trapped inside.

In addition to the great generosity of those who have supported my excavations, many individuals and institutions have kindly assisted with advice or by granting me reproductive permissions. I am grateful to Robert Roberts and Goodall's for granting permission to reproduce their adverts, and I am indebted to Unilever and to Freemans Confectionary Ltd for permission to reproduce the adverts for Bovril and for Huntley and Palmer's biscuits. Robert Opie has given his time in helpful discussions, and the staff of the History of Advertising Trust have assisted greatly, not least by supplying images. I thank Kylie for supplying the old photo of Marshbrook post office, and the staff of Shrewsbury record office and archivist of King's College, Cambridge, for all their help when I consulted their collections. Rupert Acton generously allowed me to cite unpublished materials; Gudrun Warren found the photo of Kendall, and the Dean and Chapter of Norwich Cathedral kindly granted me permission to reproduce it. My colleagues Emma Griffin, Tony Howe and Steve Cherry offered much help. Finally, I am grateful to the committee of the Centre of East Anglian Studies for voting to grant a subvention towards the cost of production, and to the editors and production team at Oxbow for putting the book together.

About the author

Dr Tom Licence is a Senior Lecturer in History at the University of East Anglia, a Fellow of the Royal Historical Society and a Fellow of the Society of Antiquaries. His previous books have been published with Oxford University Press and Boydell. Dr Licence lives on the edge of Epping Forest, in a former Victorian shop.

⇝ Introduction ⇜

THE people who lived in England before the First World War now inhabit a realm of yellow photographs. Theirs is a world fast fading from ours, yet they do not appear overly distant. Many of us can remember them as being much like ourselves. Nor is it too late for us to encounter them so intimately that we might catch ourselves worrying that we have invaded their privacy. Digging up their refuse is like peeping through the keyhole. Whatever our qualms, we must not resist such a glimpse on to the past. How far off are our grandparents in reality when we can sniff the residues of their perfume, cough medicines, and face cream? If we want to know what they bought in the village store, how they stocked the kitchen cupboard, and how they fed, pampered, and cared for themselves there is no better archive than a rubbish tip. If we wish to find out how labourers in Kent lived, compared with the postman in Shropshire, or the clergyman's family in Norfolk, we must put on our gardening gloves, clear the nettles, and dig the rich black soil. For the characters I just mentioned and thousands like them buried all the clues we need to answer our questions at the bottom of the garden. Their jumbled throwaways remain there, undisturbed and forgotten in the ground. Locating rubbish pits is like finding time capsules, full of clues about life a hundred years ago. For the historical detective each object reveals a story. A simple glass bottle can reveal what people were drinking, how a great brand emerged, or whether an inventor triumphed with a new design. An old tin tells us about advertising, household chores, or foreign imports, and even a broken plate can introduce us to the children in the Staffordshire potteries, who painted in the colours of a robin, crudely sketched on a cheap cup and saucer. Their stories must be dug from the ground because everyday minutiae rarely appear in history books. And they all contribute to the bigger story of how our great grandparents built a throwaway society from the twin foundations of packaging and mass consumption. To view this society through its rubbish is to learn how our own throwaway habits were forming.

To research this little book, I travelled round much of the country, digging up the rubbishy time capsules. Various intimate discoveries came along the way. How much beer could a postman drink? Which nursery rhymes did labourers teach their children? Did the rector and his household eat local produce? On a grander scale, the refuse pits brought to light the beginnings of a throwaway age. Revealing their secrets, they told the story of how useful things became disposable.

The idea of digging up rubbish dumps to shed light on domestic history is put to good effect on archaeological digs, where pits of this sort – 'middens' they are called – provide evidence of diet, material culture, and status. On ancient sites, archaeologists sometimes excavate and compare the contents of large numbers of middens to amass a body of evidence concerning food, clothing, and handicrafts thousands of years ago. In post-medieval research they use objects dumped in middens and cesspits to reconstruct the lives of ordinary people. Often these throwaways form dense assemblages of glass, ceramics, bones and other waste that can be linked to households whose names are recorded, but whose stories emerge only through their rubbish. A range of helpful approaches, from the popular to the more technical, can be found in the section *Further Reading*. Mostly the focus is on cities; but in the crucial period, when attitudes to waste were changing, provisions for its disposal in the cities were exceptional and far advanced beyond the systems in place across the rest of the country. City folk tend to be exceptional in any case. No book about what people threw away would be complete if it looked only at London and Birmingham.

My book comes in, not only to fill a gap, but also to open the subject to a wider readership. After all, rubbish tells many stories, of diet, medicine, brands, packaging, technology, invention, advertising, leisure, international trade, wartime hardship, the railways, literacy, class, and childhood. It would be a wasted opportunity not to have touched upon them all! Rubbish is also one vestige – a snapshot – of material culture, which is forever being renewed. Thirty years from now, the everyday objects around us, their ranks greatly thinned, will linger only in marginal spaces: in cupboards, and charity shops, and skips. Fifty years from now, they will seem strange, even alien. A few would have to be explained. Familiar things fade from our surroundings, only to surprise us when they reappear, perhaps in a dim corner, because we never admitted their passing. The stuff and material of daily life renews itself with every generation. When we dig up rubbish pits from a hundred years ago we find ourselves transported back in time by everyday objects from a forgotten era. Plunging us into the past, they speak of what our great grandparents and we have in common, of our need to eat, be well, and waste. The mould-blown sauce bottle, with its colours and air bubbles, seems reassuringly familiar. We can imagine using it: it bridges the gap. What follows now relies largely on pictures that conjure up objects thrown away. Many of these objects, paradoxically enough, have become today's collectables, because we discern in them a beauty unseen by their previous owners. It was, after all, the Victorians who formed our throwaway habits by training us to dispose of the modern equivalents of the items they themselves discarded and left for us to find. What binds their throwaway society to ours is a habit of treating categories of object, chiefly packaging, as rubbish. That habit survives and evolves.

In Victorian days, pastes, polishes, pomades, sauces, beverages, and a great host of other substances were confected at home. Mothers usually taught their daughters how to prepare them, but there was also demand for books of household hints. *Facts and Hints for Everyday Life: A Book for the Household*, by 'A. H. W.', sold 15,000 copies in the early 1870s. Its many and varied entries included recipes for jelly, hair cream, glue, brown sauce, and blacking, which was suitable for polishing, colouring, and preserving shoes or harness leather. To make blacking, a housewife or a servant could choose from three different recipes, using ingredients from the pantry, such as vinegar, treacle, and sour beer. Hair cream could be made by mixing egg white, gum arabic, and other ingredients with eau de Cologne. Unlike today's kitchen cupboard, with its shelves of packaged products, Victorian larders were packed with utilitarian vessels, for storing the ingredients, mixing the compounds, and bottling the various substances prepared at home. Glass and stoneware bottles and jars were used again and again and thrown away only when broken. *Facts and Hints* includes an entry on how to clean bottles, which recommends different methods for eradicating stains.

Richer households, of course, could afford to purchase ready-made products, which were becoming ever more affordable over the course of the nineteenth century. With colourful labels and recognisable brands, they increasingly became a feature of shopkeepers' shelves, their sales boosted by advertising. Ready-made products were labour-saving, in that they saved buyers the trouble of preparing substances at home. In an entry on 'Dyeing', the author of *Facts and Hints* remarks: 'Of old this process was a very tedious and troublesome one, requiring special attention and appliances, together with a degree of chemical knowledge not common. But now, thanks to the introduction of Judson's dyes, it is neither a long, nor an expensive, nor a difficult task.' Whether or not the author had been brainwashed by an advert for the product, hard-pressed housewives would

Figure 1. Judson's dyes, 1900s.

have valued the advice. Clothes and wicker baskets and straw hats could easily be coloured with a sixpenny bottle of dye and a basin of water. The trend in favour of labour-saving products accelerated as they multiplied towards the century's end (Fig. 1).

Wealthy households were already accustomed to consuming more than the majority. For them, sixpence was not much to spend on a bottle of dye. As well as funding their servants to purchase blacking, furniture cream, and condiments (all ready-made), they ordered luxury products, such as fine wines, Russian caviar, and Devonshire clotted cream, brought fresh to London on the early steam locomotives and sold on The Strand in ceramic jars (Fig. 2). Rather than making up hair cream from egg white, they purchased bear's grease pomades in heavy ceramic pots with transfer-printed pictures of bears on the lids. While the lower middle classes brushed their teeth with coal ash and toothbrushes carved from marshmallow roots, their social superiors attended to oral hygiene with shop-bought toothbrushes of bone, and with fine perfumed toothpaste at a shilling (twelvepence) a pot (Fig. 3). A rich

Figure 2. Advertising on ceramics. Top row, left to right: Davis, Otto of Rose, Cold Cream; Holloway's Ointment; part of the underside of a plate, showing the pattern name and diamond registration mark; Sam Clarke's Patent Pyramid Food Warmer. Middle row, left to right: Carnation toothpaste; Anchovy paste; part of a plate from Lockhart's Cocoa Rooms; Frank Cooper's Seville Marmalade; Bottom row, left to right: Poor Man's Friend (ointment, at 1s 1½d a pot); Maison Dorin, French blusher (rouge); Army & Navy, Almond Shaving Cream; Clarke's Miraculous Salve. Right: 'The Oxford' toothbrush. All discarded in London, 1880s–90s, and dumped on the Essex marshes.

lemonade drinker would sooner throw the empty bottle in the bin than take it back to the store and collect a farthing (quarter-penny) deposit, or sell it to one of the numerous street-buyers, who patrolled Victorian cities, purchasing old clothes, rags, skins, bones, grease, and bottles. Poorer families and rural households were more likely to make their own lemonade. They would have cleaned their bottles and kept them for re-filling. For all these reasons, the rich discarded more glass and ceramic vessels and more intact vessels than the poor. To the rich, vessels were disposable packaging. To poorer people or

Figure 3. Bunter's advert, showing the range of packaged products sold to those who could afford to worry about dental hygiene. 1890s.

people in the countryside where products were harder to obtain, bottles and jars possessed intrinsic value.

This difference was clearly reflected in the composition of London's rubbish. Take, for example, two unsorted samples analysed by weight, one from the poor area of St Pancras in 1889, the other from the rich borough of Kensington and Chelsea in 1892. In both, the bulk component was the remnants of household fires in the form of ash and burnt bits of coal (90% by weight at St Pancras, 80% in Kensington). But in Kensington, half of the ten percent difference was made up of bottles and glass (5% by weight in Kensington, compared with a mere 0.3% in St Pancras). The other half of the difference lay in the category of paper, vegetable, and animal waste, including grease and bones (12% in Kensington, 5.2% in St Pancras). The remaining categories of rubbish, including tins and rags, were roughly comparable, and negligible.[1] These figures show that rich people's rubbish differed from poor people's rubbish in two significant respects. The rich jettisoned twice as much paper and food waste as the poor but nearly seventeen times as much waste glass. If we could travel back in time to inspect the two dust-heaps, we would see the Kensington dust-heap glinting with bottles and pullulating with better-fed rats. Compared with St Pancras, Kensington and Chelsea was already a throwaway community, whose identity as such could be defined by its treatment of glass as disposable packaging.

It should now be apparent that waste in Victorian London was disposed of twice: once when the unwanted items were thrown into the bin, for the dust-cart to collect and cart to the yard; and a second time when it was removed from the dust-yard. Both were creative processes, in that the first act of disposal transformed objects into waste, and the second either restored their functionality or endowed them with usefulness of a different kind. Armies of the poor, most of them women, their faces blackened by ash, made their living by sorting the dust-heaps and collecting anything useful in their wicker baskets. Large pieces of coal were sold to laundresses, for use in coal laundry, or to brazier makers. Vegetable and animal matter was sold as manure or feed for pigs and poultry. Rags were used in paper making or as hop manure. Fat and marrow were sold to soap boilers and glue makers. Bones were crushed and sold as manure. Broken glass was sold to Swedish emery paper manufacturers. Whole bottles, tins, and larger pieces of fabric could be sold at recycling shops, sometimes known as 'rag and bottle shops'. Manufacturers of Prussian blue purchased old boots and shoes that could not be mended or used for repairs. Hardcore, including broken crockery, old pans, oyster shells and the like, was used as in-fill for road making or sea defences.[2] The purified piles of ash remaining were sold as manure in London's rural hinterland or ferried by private contractors in barge-loads down the Thames, to be mixed with clay, for brick making, in the brick-fields of Kent and Essex. The barges returned laden with bricks to build the metropolis, rising, ever phoenix-like, from the flames of its own ash.

As London grew, it generated more rubbish, and concerns about public hygiene grew apace. Complaining letters and lawsuits targeted the dust-yards, which could scarcely be kept apart from the accommodation of the city's expanding population. Attention was drawn to the vermin, the stench, and the miasmas. In Nottingham, in 1874, Albert Fryer responded by patenting 'The Destructor', the first engine for the wholesale incineration of waste. The following year, The Public Health Act required every household to place its refuse in a moveable receptacle called a dustbin, and it entrusted local authorities with the responsibility of regular removal and disposal. Health issues aside, it was no longer practical to sort through piles of rubbish being amassed on this scale. Nor was it profitable: for the steady growth of affluence had shrunk the market for street buyers and recycling shops. Accordingly, from the mid 1870s, London boroughs managed their waste by incineration or landfill or both. In 1904, sixteen boroughs including Kensington and St Pancras were using destructors, but it was cheaper, where possible, to dump the refuse unsorted. The fleet of barges that had once carried dust now conveyed rubbish, some of it burnt, to deposit on the marshes at the mouths of the Thames, Swale, and Medway (Figs 4 and 5). Some was purchased by brickyards to fill old clay pits. The rest was used to consolidate or raise the level of low-lying land. In his 1911 book, *Town Scavenging and Refuse Disposal*, Mr Watson remarked that it was a very cheap method of disposal: 'all that is required is a small wharf'.[3] The wooden and concrete piles of such a wharf can still be seen on the seaward side of the sea wall between Two-Tree Island and Benfleet, Essex, rising from the salt marsh (Fig. 4). Today it forms part of a nature reserve, but crockery and bottles emerging from the mud at low tide show that, for a few years in the 1890s, it was a busy tipping station. A mountainous dump above Rainham Creek was known as 'Old Man's Head'. In time the rubbish would settle down firmly and provide 'made ground', but for all the metal containers, glass jars, paper and rags no longer re-used, tin had to be mined, bottles manufactured, trees felled and pulped, and alternatives found to the organic manure previously supplied by the dust-yards.

So much for the revolution in waste management, which occurred in the final quarter of the nineteenth century. What, now, of the people who generated

Figure 4. The remains of a wharf used for offloading London rubbish in the 1890s (Thames Estuary, near Hadleigh, Essex).

Figure 5. In-destructor-ble. These items survived a destructor before being dumped near Shoeburyness and Great Wakering in Essex. 1890s. The five clay pipe bowls, made of kaolin, were originally white. Centre: a bowl moulded as a hand holding a skull. Above right: a bowl with the cartoon character Ally Sloper as the spur, and a bowl decorated with grapes. Below left: an Irish harp with a shamrock on the other side. By 1900, clay pipes were being superseded by cigarettes and briar pipes. Top left and right: dolls house jugs for the washstand and kitchen. Top centre: a marble from the middle of a solitaire board. The half melted blue-glass bottle is for poison. Below it, left, is a burnt metal button. 'The Destructor' appeared in the same decade as human cremation.

it? Did their patterns of consumption change in the same period? If we look at the diet of the poorest 10%, nothing much changed before the First World War. Meat was eaten occasionally, mostly by the head of the household, but the bulk of the diet consisted of bread and butter or dripping, potatoes and tea, supplemented in rural areas by onions, cabbages, and turnips, where agricultural labourers had vegetable plots. Well-to-do families, in contrast, had diets rich in meat, fish, eggs, milk, and sugar.[4] They also ate more pastry and puddings. Between the two extremes lay a range of social classes whose diets were generally improving on the back of upward trends in real earnings. Money wages and their purchasing capacity rose from the late 1880s and continued to rise in the years up to 1900. Meanwhile, new products were appearing and targeting new consumers. A notable company was Foster Clark's of Maidstone, founded by George Foster Clark in 1891. The Kentish firm won fame for lemonade powder and fruit juice powder, which could be added to water, to make refreshing drinks. Exploiting the sensation of the Eiffel Tower (erected in 1889), Foster Clark advertised his crystals as 'Eiffel Tower Lemonade' and 'Eiffel Tower Fruit Juices'. Some of the little bottles were embossed with pictures of the Eiffel Tower. Adverts assisted sales, like the one appearing in *Answers* magazine, in June 1899. 'A 4½d Bottle of Eiffel Tower Lemonade makes 32 Tumblers (2 Gallons) of most delicious Home-Made Lemonade' it argued. 300 bottles were given away weekly, sent to the addresses of the first fifty customers whose letters were opened each day. The lucky lottery winners would receive a little bottle, and get back their fourpence-ha'penny-worth of stamps. With its exotic associations and giveaway promotions the drink became a national brand.

Bovril was another notable success, registered at a London address in 1888. Its main strategy during the first decade was to supersede other meat extracts and beef tea. Beef tea was a nutritional drink of the poor, made from gravy and leftover meat scraps. Bovril responded by claiming to be 'the substance of beef, not the shadow'. Patriotic advertising during the Boer War enhanced its appeal among the working classes; and patriotism accompanied prestige when the company won a contract to supply Scott's polar expedition.[5] Adverts, aimed at the under-nourished, argued for Bovril's muscle- and bone-building powers. One depicts an enormous bull, gazing down sorrowfully at the tiny glass jar that contains his 'brother'. Clearly the public were meant to think that the beefy goodness of an entire bull was contained in that same tiny jar. Adverts in the early 1910s argued, on the authority of 'independent scientific experiments', that Bovril built up muscle, bone, and flesh in the proportion of 10–20 times the amount taken. There were also Bovril competitions, with themes on nutrition and health. Undoubtedly the most remarkable gimmick, which aroused immense public interest, was the flight of the Bovril Airship in the London area in 1913. One side proclaimed 'Give him Bovril', the other 'Give her Bovril'. The new marketing strategies brought an enormous increase in sales. More than 1,250,000 bottles were sold in the first five months of 1914. Like Foster Clark's bottles, they were not of a size or shape that commended re-use, so the empties went straight into the bin (Fig. 6).

Such is the story of how food preparation at home came to involve disposable vessels. Making lemonade had required only pans and re-usable bottles. Brewing up beef tea required no more than a saucepan. Foster Clark, Bovril, and a host of lesser firms brought disposable glassware into these processes. The same was increasingly true of other successful companies. Tea and coffee had long been weighed out in the store and sold in paper bags, but in the 1890s bottled tea and coffee extract came into vogue. Lipton's cornered the bottled tea market with patriotic advertising campaigns. The firm began trading tea in 1889, and, in 1892, branched out into jam, to compete with other manufacturers of jams, marmalades, jellies, and preserves, such as Crosse and Blackwell and Robertsons. Shop-bought jam vied with the home-made variety; and although jars were still re-used, consumers – now purchasing more jam – needed fewer. In any case, Mrs Stoney's promotional booklet of 1910, *A Simple Method of Bottling Fruit at Home*, promoted the use of patent glassware. 'Many crude methods of rendering bottles and jars air-tight are often practised, but it is more economical and effective', she wrote, 'to lay in a stock of reliable bottles specially made for the purpose'. For the serious jam-bottler, with cash to spare, she recommended a patent type by Mathias of Liverpool, with a glass stopper, rubber seal, and metal screw-on fastener.[6] Designed to be re-usable, patent glassware played its own, modest, part in consigning other jars to the bin. Bins were also beginning to fill with disposable tins. In 1886, the mustard makers, Colman's of Norwich, brought in tiny oval tins, priced at one penny, called 'penny ovals'. Convenient for picnics, they too generated waste. In 1900, Oxo appeared – another branded meat extract sold in disposable bottles and tins. Vim's arrival in 1904 saved housemaids the trouble of preparing scouring soap, but the tall, perforated tins, once empty, were certainly not worth saving. *Facts and Hints* advised that oxalic acid kept in a bottle labelled 'Poison' be used for cleaning brass. But Brasso's arrival in 1905 consigned such bottles to the dustbin, introducing disposable bottles of ferrous tin-alloy. Over the same decade, cheaper boot polish in bottles and tins removed a need to store sour beer and other ingredients for blacking.

Figure 6. Muscular Bovril bottles, destined for the dustbin. 1900s. Reproduced with the permission of Unilever.

As food and household commodities became more affordable, consumption rose among those on lower incomes, and a mass market emerged. Purveyors of everything from fizzy drinks to marmalade, face cream, and quack cures turned to advertising, to make their competing claims. Packaging was the most immediate form of advertising because it encouraged consumers to connect with a product at the instant of purchase. Names and claims could be embossed on the bottles, transfer-printed upon stoneware vessels, or emblazoned on colourful labels. An increasingly literate public could read them too; or, at least, they might recognise the trademark Eiffel Tower, embossed on the earlier bottles sold by Foster Clark, or the unmistakeable bull's head of Colman's mustard. No wonder, then, that the race had been on, to manufacture glassware more efficiently, as patent bottle moulds of the Victorian age gave way to semi-automatic machines in the early 1900s. In the end, it was the US inventor Michael Owens who made the breakthrough. Owens' genius was harnessed to the wallet of a glassworks owner, E. D. Libbey, whose ever-growing order books demanded innovation. While the hard-pressed Libbey churned out more and more bottles, Owens, the inventor, sat up late at his desk, sketching ever more elaborate, many-armed machines. Some of them would have puzzled even Heath Robinson, but Libbey kept investing, confident in the knowledge that Owens had invented semi-automatic machines to manufacture light bulbs, lamp chimneys, and drinking glasses. In 1903, the first fully automatic bottle machine was built to his specifications. Two years later, a commercial model was offered for production and licence internationally. The 'A', as it was known, was shipped to England and unveiled in Manchester in 1905. At that date, your typical glassworks might have employed six workers (men and boys) to make 2,880 pint-sized beer bottles in 24 hours. The 'A' could produce 17,280 and needed only two men, on twelve-hour shifts. Owens' unsleeping automaton churned out an endless stream of bottles and countered the workers' complaints of inevitable redundancies with the moral advantage of eliminating child labour.[7] Improvements followed, and by 1912, Owens was marketing a machine capable of producing 50 bottles a minute, or 72,000 a day.

Bovril, up to that point, had been grinding up its cows faster than it could bottle them: or, to say the least, its ranching operations in Australia and the Argentine were outpacing the technology of packaging. Now, with the bottling machines, just before World War I, the company switched to automated manufacture, concurrent with its massive marketing drive of 1913–14. Glassworks resistant to the new technology, or unable to afford it, lost their contracts. Such was the pace of change that most of the million and a quarter Bovril bottles sold in the early months of 1914 may have been made in automated bottle machines. Yet very few of the people enjoying their Bovril would have noticed the evidence of this packaging revolution on their table tops. In most respects, the small brown bottles were exactly the same, except that the mould seam of machine-made bottles extended through the lip (where it would have been covered by a paper label). Here, they differed from bottles blown in moulds or made in earlier, semi-automated machines, for those had to be hand-finished by 'tooling' the lip. Indeed the presence of a seam running through the lip of the bottle is one of the key means of identifying bottles made in automatic bottling machines. The same tiny difference appeared, at this time, in Foster Clark's bottles and countless others, including sauces, beers, and jam jars. By 1915, the majority of these types of vessel were machine-made. It was the subtlest revolution in the apparatus of the pantry.

A comparable revolution has been occurring in the last few decades, with many household products switching from glass to plastic. No longer is it common to smash a Lucozade bottle, or a bottle of HP Sauce, brown sauce, or Tomato Ketchup, or a jar of Vicks Vaporub, Marmite, and many kinds of honey. All now retail in plastic, even squeezable plastic, so that we don't have to shake and whack the bottles. For a while, glass and plastic bottles containing the same product will appear side-by-side on the shelves as a changeover takes place; and a similar phenomenon occurred in the 1910s, when batches of hand-made bottles were stocked interchangeably with machine-made ones. Mass-produced glass had been superseding stoneware, which was the preferred packaging for glues, pastes, polishes, blacking, inks, and ginger beer throughout the nineteenth century. Already in the 1900s, the wide-mouthed stoneware bottles for blacking had given way to glass ones and tins of boot polish. In the same decade, the Stephenson brothers of Bradford marketed their famous furniture cream in cylindrical glass, in preference to the cream-coloured stoneware bottles familiar to Victorian housemaids, which rarely occur after 1910. Virol, a nourishing food of bone marrow, sold in transfer-printed stoneware jars, began to appear in brown glass jars, modelled on the same design and embossed with the same lettering. In the early 1910s, the stoneware and glass jars and were sold side-by-side and both appeared in adverts, but the latter prevailed. In the instance of face creams and toothpastes, transfer-printed ceramic pots yielded to milk glass jars with screw-on lids from the early 1910s. Tins and cans competed with glass and stoneware alike. Tins of shoe polish of the sort we use today revolutionised the packaging of that commodity when they appeared in the 1900s. Soon, bottled polish seemed outmoded and messy to boot. Certain designs of glassware, such as the lemonade bottle with a marble in its neck to act as a valve and a stopper, could not be made in machines and disappeared. No longer could children obtain the double thrill of smashing a bottle and liberating the marble. In throwaway terms, a dump from 1900 would contain hand-finished bottles in glass and stoneware, but a dump from 1918 would contain mostly machine-made bottles, few if any items of stoneware, except for jam jars, and many more cans and tins.

Patterns of food preparation changed with the packaging revolution, because it removed the need for that array of bowls, jugs, and sundry vessels, useful in mixing, storing, and collecting ingredients measured out in the shop. Edwardian households discarded redundant vessels to free up their shelves for hordes of packaged products. Gradually, the furniture of the pantry came to resemble the stock of the village store. Re-usable containers became less prominent, while disposable ones came and went. The process of deciding what to keep and what to discard became less conscious. In the pantry envisaged by the author of *Facts and Hints*, vessels had been receptacles, containing ingredients. On the eve of the First World War, vessels were packaging, containing consumables. It was the manufacturers of the contents who decided that containers should be thrown away. Customers merely had to execute their decision. Previously, the kitchen cupboard had fed the human stomach. Now, it increasingly filled up the dustbin. In cities and towns, waste management evolved from systems established in the Victorian era, although incineration would yield to landfill in the struggle for cost-efficiency. In rural areas, organised disposal was a luxury usually arranged by the local Women's Institute or a conscientious landowner, who might provide the facility of a horse-drawn cart and a disused quarry as a tipping ground. Such provisions were laborious, sporadic, and inadequate. Many rural households dealt with waste in the age-old fashion, re-using it or tipping as appropriate. Scraps useless for cooking went to the pigs or chickens. Other organic rubbish, along with ash from the fire and dirt swept from the floor, went on the vegetable patch or was spread on the fields. Anything combustible was burned. Everything else, if it could not be recycled, was used to fill holes or tipped on useless ground. No one, given a choice, wanted to struggle very far with buckets of broken crockery and tins, so the tipping area was usually no more than twenty or thirty yards from the kitchen door. Sometimes, it belonged to someone other than the householder. For centuries, this pattern of disposal generated little waste and complaint. Then came the era of mass consumption and disposable packaging.

In 1933, The SCAPA Society, For the Prevention of Disfigurement in Town and Country, published a study concerning the disposal of domestic refuse in rural areas.[8] Unsightly piles of rubbish were spoiling the countryside, and the society intended to determine how much tipping occurred and what could be done to prevent it. Inside the booklet, they reproduced a photo showing a small pile of rubbish in a wood. Below it was the caption, 'What we don't want'. SCAPA had been founded to check the abuses of advertising. Now it was turning its attention to a problem which advertising had helped create. To research domestic tipping, the society distributed 4,000 questionnaires to Womens' Institutes in 29 English and Welsh counties. About a quarter were returned. Organised collection of refuse by a local authority or voluntary organisation, such as the WI, was reported in 50% of the returns, though it was rare in sparsely populated areas. 37% reported individual disposal, where each household made arrangements. Comments on the latter included: 'Thrown into a wood by the roadside or over the other fellow's hedge'; 'Tins thrown into holes to help fill them up'; 'There are corners in nearly every lane where rubbish and old tins are thrown because too much trouble to take them to the dump'; and, 'in more remote parts of the village the rubbish is surreptitiously dumped in the ditches or on the commons'. Most of those respondents whose comments were cited frowned upon casual tipping not because it was wasteful but because it cultivated vermin and unsightliness. No one at SCAPA asked whether items should have been thrown away in the first place. Their concern was how to rid pleasant England of its throwaways. People, nevertheless, still regarded rubbish as a resource, as the secretary of the WI in Somerset revealed inadvertently. Residents of her village tipped in a quarry in a wood, but 'trespassers' would uncover it, looking for jam jars, white wine bottles, and scrap metal. Jam and wine were still commonly made at home in rural areas, so there was demand for jars and wine bottles. Children could also earn pocket money by returning beer and fizzy drinks bottles to the store and collecting the deposit. Even so, more and more vessels were being made, and more were ending up in the ground (Figs 7 and 8).

The research underlying this book advances from the premise that a throwaway society can be studied through its rubbish. Samples had to be obtained – and not just any samples but ones from different parts of the country and different social settings. All these samples had to relate to the period of the burgeoning mass market and the packaging revolution, that is

Figure 7. Not all rubbish lasts in the ground. Tins for Pontefract cakes, tooth powder, soup, propelling pencil leads, and gramophone needles, along with cigarette packets, plant food, and Reckitt's bag blue. 1900s–1920s.

the period roughly from 1875 to 1914; and they all had to come from rural areas if they were to provide insights into individual households. The great communal rubbish dumps of towns and cities are certainly interesting, and since my first forays in 1986 I have learned much from investigating them. But their contents were all thrown together and depersonalized. Individual pits at the bottoms of rural gardens contain only what single households threw away. Furthermore, we already know about the throwaway habits of people in the towns and cities, but it is less clear to what extent and when familiar habits took hold in the countryside. Only when country people were discarding the packaging that turns up in great municipal refuse tips can we argue for the transition to a throwaway society. So I set out to find the sorts of rubbish pits that annoyed SCAPA. Between 2009 and 2012, various sites came to my

Figure 8. More packaging that would not have lasted. The proliferation of biscuits during the late nineteenth century generated much waste paper and card. Huntley & Palmer advert of c. 1900, reproduced with permission of Freeman's Confectionary Supplies Ltd.

attention, and I excavated three. Each tells its tales, to be woven into the story. The first comprised a series of pits in a chalky outcrop, to the rear of labourers' cottages in Guston, Kent. Deposits dated from 1870 to 1920. The second belonged to a post office in Marshbrook, Shropshire. From about 1910, the postman dumped his rubbish on a patch behind the pigsty. The third site was the brick-lined cesspit of the privy at Hempstead rectory, near Stalham in Norfolk. The new rector had filled it in with rubble and domestic rubbish in 1895. Here were three sites from different parts of England and different social contexts. In each instance, a picture began to appear. These were some of the people that built a consumer society.

Notes

1. Ralph Turvey, 'Economic growth and domestic refuse in London', in *LSE on Social Science*, ed. Helen Sasson and Derek Diamond (London, 1996), pp. 217–35.
2. L. Herbert, *Centenary History of Waste and Waste Management in London and South East England*, The Chartered Institute of Wastes Management (London, 2009), p. 7.
3. Hugh S. Watson, *Town Scavenging and Refuse Disposal: a Hand Book of Modern Practice* (London, 1911), p. 26.
4. Michael Nelson, 'Social-class trends in British diet, 1860–1980', in *Food, Diet and Economic Change Past and Present*, ed. C. Geissler and D. J. Oddy (Leicester, London, and New York, 1993), pp. 101–120, at pp. 102–3.
5. P. Hadley, *The History of Bovril Advertising* (London, 1970), pp. 8–25.
6. J. Stoney, *A Simple Method of Bottling Fruit at Home, with Recipes for Home-made Jams, Wines and Pickles by Mrs Stoney* (Stafford, 1910), p. 7.
7. Q. R. Skrabec, Jr, *Michael Owens and the Glass Industry* (Gretna, Louisiana, 2007).
8. SCAPA was the Society for Checking the Abuses of Public Advertising. See Ethel Bright Ashford and Humphrey Baker, *Rural Refuse and its Disposal*, The SCAPA Society, For the Prevention of Disfigurement in Town and Country (Letchworth Garden City, 1933).

⇜ 1. Labourers' Cottages in Kent ⇝

PEAR Tree Cottage in Guston is a long, low building of seventeenth-century date, with a third of an acre of garden, mostly to the rear. Formerly it was divided into four tiny cottages. The different treatment of their outer walls, and also their different floor levels, can still be seen on the property (Fig. 9). Ordnance Survey maps from the late Victorian period reveal that this row of cottages shared half an acre with two cottages next door. A few outbuildings are visible on the maps, as is a well in the front yard. In the 1940s the cottages were known as 'Well Cottages'. Census returns show that most of the people living in the lane were agricultural labourers, but it is hard to tell exactly where

Figure 9. Pear Tree Cottage, Guston, pictured from the rear.

they lived. Today, the garden of Pear Tree Cottage, with its vegetable plots and beehives, rises on a steepish incline towards a chalky ridge. In rural areas, chalk was dug to make mortar and whitewash, and the inhabitants of Well Cottages exploited it. All along the ridge there was evidence of chalk digging, with one hole cut more than nine feet deep. The author of *Facts and Hints* advised that a little 'blue' (a product for whitening laundry) should be mixed with the lime used for whitewash to bring out the brilliance of the white.[1] When the tenants had dug enough chalk, they filled their pits with rubbish. During my excavations, I sampled three, which opened a window on to a dimly familiar world. The first contained a clayey fill packed with broken crockery and broken bottles dating to the last quarter of the nineteenth century. The second pit, partly overlying the first, contained many more intact bottles and tins (Fig. 10). A cup commemorating Queen Victoria's Diamond Jubilee dated the deposit later than 1897, and a bottle for 'Lipton's Limited' dated it after 1898, but no object suggested a date later than 1910.[2] The third pit was more than nine feet deep and contained rubbish from the 1910s. In one of the lowest levels was a cache of rubbish in a rusty bucket, which included five bottles for

Figure 10. Bottles and jars from the second pit. The brown jar at the front held cream.

Foster Clark's fruit juice. Four were embossed 'Foster Clark Ltd', but one had 'Foster Clark & Co', which suggested that these bottles were manufactured *c.* 1910, when the firm became a private company. Upper layers dated from the mid-late 1910s. It was impossible to tell whether the tenants of the different cottages shared these dumps or had one each.

Guston had no organised waste collection until 1934, but we must start by asking what the labourers threw away in the late Victorian period. Most of the contents of the first pit had been smashed before going into the ground. The crockery was utilitarian, almost without exception, consisting of plates, bowls, jugs, mugs, candlesticks, wash bowls, pudding basins, serving dishes, teacups, and chamber pots. They were pottery rather than the more costly porcelain, and all fell into one of three categories: 1) off-white, plain undecorated pottery; 2) Mocha ware/'banded ware', which was cheaply manufactured and decorated with vaguely foliate patterns; and 3) transfer-printed ware, mostly in blue, predominantly 'willow pattern' (Fig. 11). These varieties of crockery were inexpensive, whether second-hand or new. Though most bottles had been smashed, the bases revealed that about a quarter were moulded specimens with scars left by the glass blower's pontil rod. Manufactured before the 1870s, the bottles must have been re-used many times, then broken and dumped with the later material. Sometimes, early bottles were sealed with the name of the purveyor by stamping it in a blob of glass attached to the bottle's shoulder when it was still hot. Such a seal was found among the refuse, having separated from a large, rectangular, mould-blown bottle of 'aqua' glass (that is, glass with a greenish tinge). It bore the name 'Payne & Son, 328, Regent St' (Fig. 12). In a directory of 1841, George Payne & Son are listed at 328 Regent St, as owning a 'tea establishment'. The bottle was indeed of a sort that might have contained dried tea.[3] After decades on the pantry shelf its working life had ended, probably because it broke.

Quantities of limpet shells in this deposit had been collected from the coast two miles away. Limpets clinging to rocks near the mark of high tide grow pointier shells because they develop larger muscles to survive the crashing waves, whereas the shells of limpets lower down the beach are flatter. Tenants of Well Cottages brought back both, possibly from Dover or St Margaret's Bay. Dozens of shells in their refuse, along with occasional oyster shells, indicated that limpets were a dietary supplement. Bones were not always discarded, but there were a few pork and mutton bones. Under layers of glass, crockery, and shells was an upturned earthenware tub buried beside an upturned metal pail (Fig. 13). The tub was broken; the pail was worn thin and holed. Both had

Figure 11 (above). Mocha ware, willow pattern, and other crockery from Guston.

Figure 12 (right). A glass seal from a bottle sold by Payne & Son, 328 Regent St. c. 1840s.

Figure 13. Earthenware tub, left; metal tub, right. Both were full of rubbish. 1870s.

done their final service conveying rubbish from the kitchen door. Careful excavation of the contents uncovered parts of a cup and saucer, some in the tub, some in the pail. Part of a set, they were made of finer pottery, to resemble porcelain. They showed a robin on a bough of holly, with the colours painted in, clumsily, by factory children. Cup and saucer, certainly, should be placed at the better end of that cheap assortment of tableware. The decoration hinted that they came out at Christmas.

Were the two tubs a Christmas deposit? The contents did not suggest otherwise. There were three cups and one saucer showing the robin on the sprig of holly, along with remnants of a fine, stemmed wine glass; a goblet which might have held wine, posset, or punch; a hand-painted egg cup, crudely decorated with foliage resembling holly or ivy, and quantities of bottle glass from wine bottles (Fig. 14). Two unusual bottles had been put in with this rubbish intact (Fig. 15). One was a soda water bottle moulded as a round-bottomed cylinder. Bottles of this shape, although less common than the egg-shaped kind, were designed with rounded bottoms for the same reason: to

24

Figure 14. A robin on a sprig (cups and saucer). Egg cup, glasses, and a tiny doll.

Figure 15. Goffe's soda water (round-bottomed cylinder) and sauce bottle. 1870s.

force proprietors to store them on their side. Fizzy drinks in upright bottles tended to go flat, because their corks would dry out and shrink, allowing the gas to escape. The simplest way to prevent this was to keep the cork in contact with the liquid. Egg-shaped and round-bottomed bottles guaranteed the fizz and took the annoying gamble out of buying carbonated drinks.

The specimen thrown out with the Christmas refuse had come all the way from Birmingham. It bore the simple advert, 'Goffe / Birm'm / Genuine / Soda Water'. Jim Goffe established his manufactory in 1837 and appears in directories at an address in Duke Street. By the 1860s, he was trading on the testimonials of Dr Alfred Hill and Dr Francis Wrightson, lecturers in chemistry. Hill had inspected the machinery used in making soda waters and artificial mineral waters, which Goffe called 'Carlsbad', 'Seltzer', and 'Vichy' after famous European mineral spas, and was pleased to find that its working parts were thickly coated in silver, 'to prevent contamination of the Waters by injurious metals'. He noted: 'The water is the purest afforded by the red sandstone formation … and is further improved by a large admixture of Distilled Water' (which medical authorities at the time deemed effective against cancer).[4] Wrightson remarked, 'The Aërated Waters are very highly charged with Carbonic Acid Gas … by means of a powerful steam engine'. Goffe's trademark depicted two bottles: an egg-shaped one and a round-bottomed cylinder like the one in the tub.[5] The other intact bottle was a decoratively moulded sauce with a needle-thin neck. It too was a luxury. What the two bottles have in common are improved features that discouraged re-use. Nothing could be done with a round-bottomed bottle once the soda was gone, or with a narrow-necked container once the sauce had dribbled out. Though we think of it as a modern phenomenon, obsolescence attended the design, and both were discarded intact.

The Christmas deposit dated from the 1870s and was overlain by rubbish from later decades. Along the ridge, a second pit contained refuse from the 1900s with a similar array of transfer-printed crockery, but no Mocha ware. Part of a stoneware hot-water bottle carried the name of a family grocer, 'Frederick Finn & Sons, Ltd, Canterbury'. A souvenir cup bore a transfer-printed image of Canterbury cathedral. Other souvenirs included a jug with Queen Victoria's head, and a jubilee cup from 1897. Five bottles for 'Mrs Winslow's Soothing Syrup' once contained a compound of morphine for putting babies to sleep. For decades it had sold well in the USA and in England, but the author of *Facts and Hints* issues a terrifying warning: 'Opium is too extensively used by idle and ignorant persons in charge of children to save them the trouble of doing their duty as nurses. All the "soothing" messes sold for giving to children are more or

Figure 16. A wasted childhood. Alphabet and nursery rhyme cups, dolls, etc.

less impregnated with laudanum, which always injures and often proves fatal'.[6] Morphine soothers later came to be known as 'baby killers'.

Childhood at Guston was not quite so bleak. Toys amid the rubbish included the cheap doll's head, headless toy milkmaid, cockerel in imitation Parian ware, and the blue-glass hen on a nest shown in Figure 16. Most of these toys related to the rural life the children must have known. A child's cup shows a little boy running with a hoop. Another illustrates a bird, with the word 'WREN'. The educational philosophy here was akin to the 'object lessons' infants took at school, with a series of classes given over to studying different objects. Object lessons at Bergh Apton school in Norfolk, for the year 1884–5, included: wheat, barley, maize, oats, sheep, mouse, horse, goat, frog, elephant, duck, pigeon, pheasant, partridge, umbrella, tables, lamp, coins, coal, chairs, primroses, and buttercups – but not wren.[7] Two nursery-rhyme cups, from a set, depicted verses from 'This is the house that Jack built'.

The first carries a verse and portrays the cat and the dog, transfer-printed in green. Part is still legible, so we can fill in the rest (in italics):

THIS IS THE DOG
THAT WORRIED THE CAT
*THAT KILLE*D THE RAT
THAT ATE THE MALT
THAT LAY IN THE HOUSE
THAT JACK BUILT

The other cup, depicting the cockerel and the priest, printed in brown, explains:

THIS IS THE COCK
THAT CROWED IN THE MORN
THAT WAKED THE PRIEST
ALL SHAVEN AND SHORN …

We may not know the names of the tenants, but we know which rhymes they taught their children. Curiously, the cups are of pearl ware of the 1840s or 1850s and must have been hand-me-downs or second-hand presents. Also in this rubbish were three broken alphabet cups, providing further evidence that the children learned to read at home. A child's slate pencil hints at writing lessons. A tiny thimble could have been used in sampler embroidery. 'Codd bottles', sealed with a marble in a rubber ring to keep the contents fizzy, had been smashed deliberately and all the marbles removed. Pieces of a dolls' tea set had been swept up and lost in the rubbish, as had a tiny doll bound with copper wire, which may have adorned a Christmas tree.

Deposits of this sort cannot tell us very much about the organic components of people's diets – the bread and butter, meat and vegetables, and the like. But dietary details are recorded in studies by Victorian social reformers. Records of meals eaten in the 1900s by North Yorkshire ironworkers, for example, reveal that they left little waste. Pickled cabbages were popular. 'The favourite kind are big red cabbages, of which four large ones pickled in a glass bottle would last the family one week, as an accompaniment to the usual fare'.[8] Such bottles lent themselves to constant re-use. Most of the food packaging from the second pit at Guston had contained products to flavour the monotony of a plain diet, such as sauces, pickles, jams, and preserves. It dated from the 1900s, when pickled cabbages bulked out the diet of the ironworkers. Two bottles advertised 'Garton's HP Sauce'; another two were embossed 'Goodall Backhouse & Co, Yorkshire Relish' (Figs 17 and 18). All were discarded intact,

Figure 17. Goodall's advert, showing sauce bottle and labelling. 1900s. (With permission from Goodall's.)

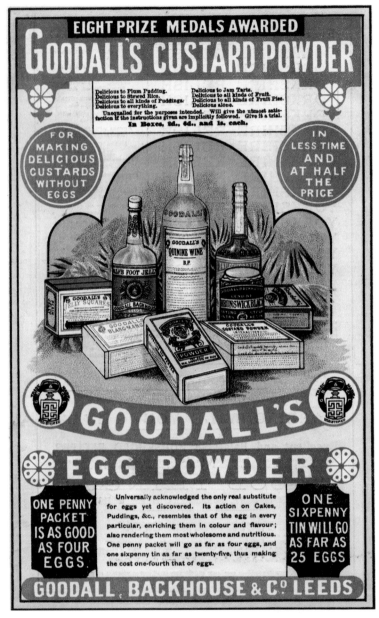

Figure 18. Goodall's advert, showing a range of products. Much of the packaging would not survive in the ground. 1900s. (With permission from Goodall's.)

with their glass stoppers. Another sauce bottle, stained red inside, was identical to one in Mr Opie's collection, labelled as Lazenby's essence of anchovies and browning for gravies. Mr Opie's bottle is stained with the same rusty red colouring inside. Jars for pickles, chutneys, and jams had been dumped intact, as had a rough, unornamented ginger jar and two earthenware cream jars. The jars could have been re-used, if the tenants had wished to re-use them – but these vessels were surplus to requirements. Egg cups and pudding bowls attest to dietary luxuries the poorest could not afford. Unlike the jars, they were thrown away only when broken.

Alcoholic drinks were not much in evidence beyond the remnants of a few wine bottles, and a solitary beer from Alfred Leney of Dover. This could indicate that the tenants generally collected their beer in a jug, or sent the children to get it from The Plough up the lane, a widespread practice at that time, which might well account for the Mocha ware jugs and mugs in the earlier deposit, which bore stamps for imperial measures. Beer, wine, and spirit bottles were returned by the same paths, so alcohol consumption generated little waste. Milk likewise required only a jug. Fizzy drinks bottles could also be returned, but not all of them were. J. W. Court, of Deal, sold mineral water in 'Codd bottles', sealed with a marble in a rubber ring. They fell foul of the children, who smashed them for the marbles. Another fizzy drinks bottle, from 'The Dover and District Mineral Water Company', was discarded intact. But a tall stoneware bottle for seltzer water of the sort commonly imported from Germany had come all the way from Passau, in Bavaria, before it was smashed and discarded. Years ago, I found a similar bottle in the mud on the South Bank of the Thames, not far from an old jetty. It bore the seal of Neiderselters in Nassau, the original mineral spa, which gave us the word 'seltzer'. This particular seal was in use between 1866 and 1880, so the bottle from the Thames was imported and probably discarded when James Goffe was making 'Seltzer' artificially in Birmingham. Returning to our later rubbish in Guston, we may not be surprised to find the Edwardian cottagers drinking Foster Clark's 'Eiffel Tower Fruit Juices'. Four intact bottles turned up in the deposit, and two broken ones – enough for 192 tumblers of fruit juice, according to the advert of 1899. This, or tea, would have filled the cups that told of the house that Jack built. The grown-ups were drinking bottled tea and coffee. Bulky oblong bottles advertised their contents: 'Liptons, London & Ceylon' (for tea), and 'Paterson's Essence, Camp Coffee & Chicory, Glasgow', and 'Branson Ltd, Coffee Extract'. All were purveyors of household brands, just like Garton's, Goodall Backhouse, and, increasingly, Foster Clark's. During the 1900s, the cottagers in Guston were switching to brands for their sauces, fruit juices, and bottled tea and coffee, but not their fizzy drinks or alcoholic beverages, which came from local manufacturers.

Writing required ink, which could be purchased from the shops either in heavy, stoneware bottles with pouring lips, for dispensing it into a desk inkwell, or in little, cheaply-made bottles, disposable inkwells themselves. Some of the latter came with recesses in the shoulder for resting the pen. Many were moulded in attractive shapes such as octagons, birdcages, cottages, and bells. Glass ones usually had burst-off lips, a feature of the cheapest bottles. Instead of applying a lip, or 'tooling' the end of the bottleneck to make it smooth, the glassblower allowed a bubble to form, which burst, allowing the bottle to be detached from the blowpipe. Simple and cheap, the method left a jagged edge which readily accommodated a rough-fitting cork and sealing wax. Burst-off lips did not only appear on inks but also on sauces, dyes, and even poisons. Foster Clark used burst-off-lip bottles at first in the 1890s, but switched to tooled-lip bottles during the 1900s. Seven cheap burst-off-lip ink bottles surfaced, intact, in the deposit, along with two small stoneware ones. These cost a penny each – the price of a light meal – and were dumped when empty. There were no master ink bottles with pouring lips – a kind of bottle used to fill desk inkwells in Victorian schools – so it is doubtful that the tenants enjoyed the luxury of an inkwell. Another stoneware bottle contained 'Glessen Blue', for mixing with whites in the wash, or indeed for mixing with whitewash (because cobalt offset yellowish hues). There was also a stoneware jar for blacking or stove polish. For Sundays at least, shirts, dresses, and shoes had to be immaculate. Another stoneware bottle, possibly for bleach, bore the mark of the Doulton potteries at Lambeth. The 'Glessen Blue' bottle had the stamp of Bourne, Denby; and a disposable cream jug displayed the name of Price of Bristol. Year on year, the potteries churned out huge numbers of utilitarian vessels of this sort, until demand dried up in the years around 1910, when manufacturers of products sold in stoneware turned to cheap glass and tins (Fig. 19).

Medicine bottles came in standard shapes with paper labels. The pharmacist wrote the contents on the label, but only the bottles survive in the ground. Branded medicines, on the other hand, were sold in embossed bottles. Evidence in this form reveals that our labourers at Guston, like many of their contemporaries, remedied stomach complaints with 'Bishop's Granular Citrate of Magnesia' and laboured to improve their health with 'Eno's Fruit Salts'. Both were widely sold in disposable glass. A blue, hexagonal bottle, with ribs down three sides, contained a substance 'NOT TO BE TAKEN'. Bottles for poisonous

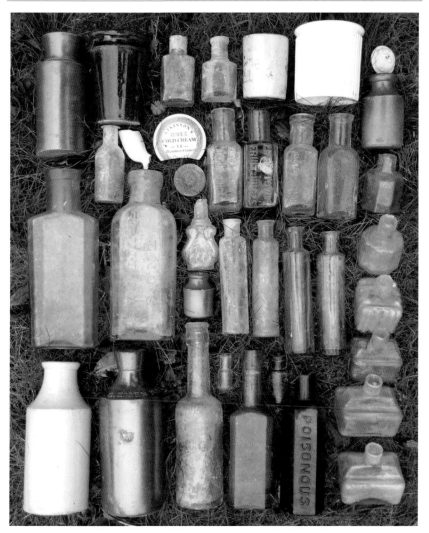

Figure 19. Bottom row, left to right: two stoneware bottles, including 'Glessen Blue'; Yorkshire relish; gravy browning; poison. Up the right hand side: a column of cheap ink bottles. Centre right: soothing syrups. Top left, a small blacking bottle.

substances were distinguished thus, with the aim of preventing people from confusing them with medicines. Perfume bottles are easily identified by their clear glass and decorative moulding. Two had been thrown away, along with a pot lid for 'Atkinson's Rose Cold Cream'. It was certainly extravagant for the tenants to purchase this at a shilling a pot, but a few luxuries of this sort do turn up in cottage dumps, showing that labourers were not always as thrifty as model budgets imply. Finally, among the rubbish in this pit, I came across a small bottle embossed with the details: 'The Singer Manufacturing Company, Extra Quality Machine Oil'. As the brand suggests, it was for oiling a sewing machine. The oily empty bottle of course could not be salvaged and went straight into the bin. Special oils for special machines were not easily concocted, particularly if their manufacturers said so! But cannier home keepers would have found oils in the pantry to keep the Singer humming. A common cottage industry, sewing merited a bit of capital investment, and it is likely that one of the women living in the cottages might have earned two or three shillings a week by mending clothes for better-off villagers.

In parts of the early pits, the crockery was packed so thickly that it resembled layers of limestone in a sedimentary deposit. Layer on layer of smashed plates and broken bowls made excavation difficult. Surely even a poltergeist or the cook from *Alice in Wonderland* could not have broken this much? George Acorn grew up in a London slum in the late Victorian period. In his memoirs, he describes how people dwelling in those overcrowded conditions, seldom with much to eat, lived at such a pitch of anxiety that outbursts of anger and flinging of crockery were commonplace. 'Cups or saucers were picked up from the table and thrown at each other', he notes, and he recalls how his mother, 'seizing a jug standing on a kind of dresser, hurled it into my father's face', judging this behaviour ordinary.[9] Whether or not plates and jugs were flung around at Guston, it is worth asking how much crockery an average family broke. Help is forthcoming in the accounts of Pearce and Plenty, a restaurant outlet in East London – where Acorn grew up – which sold large numbers of cheap meals to workmen. A typical 'penny breakfast' included a mug of steaming tea, for half a penny, and a bit of bread and butter, also at a ha'penny. Carters and lorrymen, who made an early start, were the first customers. Larger breakfasts could be had for tuppence, and a meaty dinner at midday for fivepence or sixpence. The average cost to the diner at Pearce and Plenty was less than 2d.

Now in 1902 this outlet was supplying 40,000 meals a day. We also know from their records that 100 cups and mugs were broken each day along with 40,000 plates and saucers each year, on average.[10] Hence, if Pearce and Plenty opened its doors on 310 days each year – that is, if we subtract 52 Sundays and three holidays from 365 – then it must have dished up in the region of 12,400,000 meals annually. Dividing this figure by the annual number of breakages (*i.e.* 31,000 mugs/cups, and 40,000 plates/saucers), we find that, on average, taking into account serving, eating, and washing-up, one plate or saucer was broken for every 310 meals and one cup or mug for every 400 meals. If these statistics were comparable to breakages at home, then an average family of four, eating three meals daily, every day of the year (that is 4,380 meals in total), would have broken 14 plates/saucers and 11 cups/mugs each year. Moreover, they must have suffered breakages not reckoned in Pearce and Plenty's totals, for the family also used pots, plates, jugs, and bowls for preparing and carrying food and for fetching their provisions. And the ewers, bowls, soap-dishes, brush trays, candlesticks and toothbrush holders on the washstands, the chamber pots under their beds, and the vases and teapots on the sideboard, also got knocked around. So if we allow a modest tally of 10 breakages a year in this additional category of *everything else*, then a non-violent family of four should have broken 35 utilitarian ceramic items annually. Even if every item shattered into no more than three pieces, a year's rubbish would contain over a hundred sherds of pottery.

Statistics of this sort offer a rough guide only. In reality, numbers of breakages must have varied. A large establishment such as Pearce and Plenty might well have been more careless than the average family. Richer families, on the other hand, may have upgraded their crockery now and then, or discarded whole items, or even large numbers of items from the same dinner service, when pieces in the set were broken. These statistics nevertheless do appear to tally with the quantities of crockery in the pits. For example, pit number two, which can hardly have lain open for more than a few years, contained something in the region of two hundred broken ceramic items. Lamp chimneys, drinking glasses, and utilitarian bottles were typically more fragile than plates and mugs and may have been broken more often. In the 1910s, however, the use of ceramic vessels in preparing food decreased in proportion to the growing popularity of enamelled kitchenware. Moreover by 1910 the explosion in packaged products meant that fewer plates, bowls, and jugs had to be carried to the store, pub, or market, to bring home provisions. No doubt an average family living in the 1910s broke just as many mugs and saucers as a family of the 1900s. But breakages in the additional category of *everything else* would have been fewer for those reasons. We see the change in the profile of the refuse across those decades. In short, waste from the 1900s contains more broken crockery, whereas rubbish from the 1910s contains less crockery but more 'packaging' in the form of whole bottles, tins, cans, and jars.

Pit number three, at Guston, dated from the 1910s. It was also the deepest and richest both in its contents and state of preservation. Lower layers especially lacked the oxygen needed by bacteria. Shoes survived very well in those layers, as did tins. More than ten metal buckets, packed with tins, bottles, crockery, shoes, and sundry rubbish, appeared, at various levels. Wooden buckets bound with metal hoops had been filled and dumped in the hole too. The hoops survived. A bathtub and a giant kettle met their end in similar fashion. Working people in the countryside evidently got through a lot of buckets. Zinc ones cost a shilling, which was about a twelfth of the average labourer's weekly earnings by *c.* 1900. The pattern of tipping suggests that a bucket or two would have been stationed at the back door for rubbish before being carried to the pit when full. Older buckets performed such a role as their last call of duty. As expected, this larger dump from the 1910s contained less crockery than the early ones. Less crockery was used by that date, and less was broken. Still, mixing bowls and pudding bowls, jugs, plates, cups, saucers, basins, chamber pots, candlesticks, and flower pots were all present in pieces, along with a teapot or two. Crockery for the table was of a cheaper sort: plain white or transfer-printed in blue, mostly. Bottles and tins were more numerous in this deposit than in the earlier pits, though it did hold a larger sample of rubbish. Ceramic containers, notably jam and marmalade jars, were present as before; but stoneware bottles had vanished. Below are the numbers of intact vessels found in the pit of the 1900s, and in the pit of the 1910s.

	1900s pit	*1910s pit*
Glass bottles	68	101
Ceramic jars	6	4
Stoneware bottles	7	0

What were the tenants consuming in the early 1910s? Tins from near the bottom preserved names and particulars of their contents. Two had contained 'Broma-cocoa', sold by the Co-operative Wholesale Society Ltd, used for making hot chocolate and also in baking. They commended its 'Great strength, exquisite flavour'. Another tin had contained Lipton's golden syrup, 'by appointment to His Majesty the King'. It displayed a picture of Lipton's head offices in London, with early motor vehicles in the foreground and a horse-drawn tram. This and broken pudding bowls hint that the tenants enjoyed sponge pudding, but the tin had been re-used for mixing green paint as a final duty before it was dumped. Jam and marmalade jars were not as numerous as they sometimes are in deposits of this date. One, from 'The Army and

Figure 20. Army and Navy jam jar and Keiller marmalade jar. (Third pit, Guston.)

Navy Co-operative Society Ltd', was re-used more than once, judging by its condition. I once unearthed another in a large city dump outside Canterbury, which had been used for mixing white paint. The jar in the pit at Guston turned up in the same bucket as one for James Keiller and Sons' 'Dundee Marmalade' (Fig. 20). The latter jar, made by Maling of Newcastle, showed no obvious signs of wear, unlike the Army and Navy jar. Perhaps they were discarded in a clear out. Useful preserves jars and large fruit jars were found unbroken near the bottom of the hole, despite their serviceability. A printed cream pot advertised 'Devonshire Clotted Cream, Fresh Daily at Tucker's, 287 Strand' (Fig. 21). Though flawless, it had spent decades on a shelf. The poulterer J. Tucker is listed at that address in 1882 and 1884 but had gone by 1891, so that pot was more than twenty years old when someone threw it away. Part of a similar cream pot turned up in the first pit, with refuse from the 1880s. The rear displayed a picture of a steam train, the vehicle that had transported the cream to London and onwards to Kent (Fig. 22). In the 1880s, the tenants would have enjoyed Devonshire cream sent down from London. Perhaps Tucker's pot had been sitting in a cupboard somewhere ever

Figure 21 (above). Tucker's Devonshire Clotted Cream pot, 1880s. Wine bottles, c. 1910.

Figure 22 (left). Clotted cream pot, rear base, with trade mark Devon steam train, 1880s.

since. Chickens pecking around the garden supplied fresh eggs, as they still do today at the cottage. Every pit contained at least one broken eggcup.

Foster Clark's bottles (with long necks – the type used in the 1900s)

38

Figure 23. Foster Clark's bottles, showing their evolution. Far left: a burst-off-lip bottle, dating before 1900; Centre: three long-necked bottles from the 1900s; Far right: a short-necked specimen, c. 1910.

appeared in the second pit, and more of his bottles (with shorter necks – introduced before 1910) were found near the bottom of pit number three (Fig. 23). Whoever filled the second pit also drank from 'Codd bottles' sold by J. W. Court of Deal. Identical bottles sold by J. W. Court and 'J. W. Court & Sons' were found near the bottom of the third pit. Unlike those in the earlier pit, they had not been broken for the marbles, but perhaps children could not get at them in the bottom of a very deep hole. John Wyatt Court, a publican in Deal, was 67 years old for the 1911 census. His eldest son, Edward, was 38. Three bottles from his firm were the only evidence from this pit that the tenants enjoyed fizzy drinks. Beer bottles were more numerous and, again, from local firms (Fig. 24). Three came from 'Leney & Co', Dover, and one from 'Ind, Coope and Co' at the Romford brewery in Essex. Wear-marks on its base revealed that the Romford bottle had been filled more than once during its travels. Evidence of whisky from the second pit came in the form of a bottle shaped like a pumpkin seed. These distinctive bottles were known as 'pumpkin seed flasks'. Whisky bottles dug up in the third pit included one from Dewars', Perth, and another, from James Buchanan & Co, which advertised 'Finest Old Highland Malt Whisky' (Fig. 25). All lay near the bottom of the hole, a fact that may be significant. In 1909, the chancellor Lloyd George raised distillery licence fees and increased the rate of

Figure 24. Left: beer bottles from Leney and Ind, Coope & Co. Centre: so-called 'Codd bottles', from J. W. Court and J. W. Court and Sons, Deal.

duty on spirits by a third, arguing for temperance. By 1910, total UK spirit consumption had fallen by a third. Attacks on the industry in 1914 and 1915 also dispirited drinkers.[11] Drunkenness and violence were problems in some households. In 1916, tenants in the cottages kept dangerous dogs which were not under control and were a menace in lambing season. The dogs were not licensed, and the parish clerk was asked to see to the matter.[12] Wine bottles were mostly confined to the bottom of the hole, where half a dozen jostled with the whisky bottles. Children could have removed large empties of this sort from higher layers of refuse.

One significant difference in the rubbish from the 1910s was the total absence of bottles for tea, coffee, and sauce. We have to assume that these items, in shop-bought bottles, were no longer on the menu. On the other hand, the cottagers had discovered Bovril, which could serve both as a hot drink and flavouring for food. More than 40 Bovril bottles came out of the

Figure 25. Whisky bottles etc., early 1910s. Note the billycan, bottom centre, and leather boot, top centre left. The object resting on the whisky bottles, bottom right, is a pocket watch. (Third pit, Guston.)

hole, and others had broken in the ground. Four came out of one bucket. All were machine-made, and they first appeared in a middle layer of refuse, datable to 1913 or 1914. At the cottages in Guston, consumption of Bovril clearly began at the time of the great marketing drive and continued on an industrial scale. Indeed, the labourers were the company's target market: maybe short of meat, but needing muscle. During the first few months of the war in 1914, beef prices rose by 16%. The price of lower quality beef, however, rose by 30% because it was being purchased for the armed forces. In 1915, taxes were raised on tea, coffee, and cocoa, while U-boats continued to sink Britain's merchant fleet.[13] Such developments could help to account for the new ascendancy of Bovril, which remained the same price all through the war, when practically everything else in the shopping basket doubled in cost.[14] A single bottle for 'Vimbos' and one for 'Oxo' show that the tenants did give alternatives a chance, but it was clear where their loyalties lay in the struggle of rival extracts whose Latinate names extolled their beefiness. Small oval tins also emerged in the refuse and may have contained Colman's mustard. Ornate barrel-shaped glass jars were replacing the ceramic pots once used for crab, shrimp, and fish pastes. The earliest I have found was registered in 1912.

Medicine bottles from the major dispensing chemists made their first appearance in the third pit. They included bottles from 'Boots Cash Chemist', 'Timothy White Ltd', and Woodward's of Nottingham. Pharmaceutical equivalents of the brands, the names of these chemists are common on containers found in middens from the 1910s when retailers were becoming more and more familiar. A little pill bottle contained a product of the 'Tabloid' range, made in Dartford by Burroughs Wellcome and Co. It proclaimed that the company had won 'over 270 awards', a tally it exceeded in 1912. 'Ephedrine Hydroch' pills and 'Diginutrin' were two medicines sold in these bottles. Alongside it, a bottle for 'Veno's Lightning Cough Cure' had smashed in the ground, showing the contrast between a traditional cure of the Victorian period, commended by a familiar name and the attributes of its contents, and novel pharmaceutical drugs with technical titles. Both kinds are still in the market today. Cosmetics included the ubiquitous 'Harlene for the Hair', a nourishing shampoo and hair-restorer. In the pits from earlier decades, cosmetics were not prominent, but they accounted for many of the vessels dumped in this one. Apart from several fancy bottles for French perfume, toilet water, and the like, most had contained cold cream or vanishing cream, which was sold in milk glass jars with screw-on lids, by perfumiers such as Pond's and the Anzora Perfumery. Pond's advertising campaign of the early 1910s helps to explain the presence of fifteen jars of this sort, which recall the more expensive pot found in the earlier pit, for Atkinson's rose cold cream, priced a shilling. Simpler than Pond's moulded jars, these suggest a cheaper imitation (Figs 26 and 27). Somebody at Guston had to care for a horse. Near the bottom of the hole was a bottle embossed, 'L. S. D. Infallible Embrocation for Horses', sold by S. and H. Harris of London. If the horse took L. S. D., rats were dosed with poison, as a poison bottle implied. Neither it nor the vet's bottle was kept for re-use. Five disposable inkwell-bottles exacerbated the throwaway trend. (See Figs 25 and 26 for an array of items.)

The wear and tear of daily life in the cottages filled that hole with echoes. The only stoneware bottle was a small flagon, holed in the side and missing its handle. Flagons of this sort, for cider or beer, were used until they broke. Old photos show labourers taking them into the fields with their lunch baskets. A billycan missing its lid, and hob-nailed boots beyond repair, told a similar story (Fig. 25). In the earlier pits, leather had decomposed, but one pit contained a pair of metal pattens, designed to raise the shoe above boggy ground or keep

Figure 26. Items from the third pit, Guston. 1910s. Along the bottom, 26 Bovrils. Above them, 12 milk glass jars with screw-on lids. Pond's and other companies employed these for cold cream.

Figure 27. Pond's ointment. c. 1910.

it dry around the cowshed (Fig. 28). I found Victorian pattens not unlike these in the dredgings of a ditch at the rear of an old farmhouse near Pett Level, East Sussex. The dredging uncovered bottles for tea, coffee extract, and Foster Clark's lemonade from the years before 1910. In the mud beside that ditch, and in the pit at Guston, were large stones and brick rubble, tossed in as garden rubbish. Household bits in the Guston pit included fragments of broken oil lamps (mostly their glass chimneys), part of a decorative picture frame, the lens from a hand-held outdoor lamp, a boot hook, a meat hook (Fig. 28), curtain rings, bone buttons (Fig. 29), and .303 cartridge cases. These

Figure 28 (left). Pattens and a meat hook.

Figure 29 (below). Bone buttons, left; and a mother of pearl button, right.

were the standard issue for British servicemen. Among the military items were two general service buttons from a great coat, one bearing Victoria's crown, the other showing a king's crown. A cap badge and buttons of a light infantry regiment bore the same bugle below Victoria's crown. They were fairly old when the pit was filled. Badge and buttons might have been swept up with the rubbish or thrown away still attached to outdated kit. They evoke labouring life on the eve of the War, transporting us two generations beyond our mid-Victorian Christmas into a different era – an era of brands and packaging.

Notes

1. *Facts and Hints*, p. 396.
2. Lipton was incorporated in 1898.
3. *Post Office London Directory, 1841, Part I*, p. 509.
4. W. T. Fernie, *Kitchen Physic* (Bristol, 1901), pp. 94–5.
5. *Post Office Directory of Birmingham, 1867*, p. 458.
6. *Facts and Hints*, p. 284.
7. Norfolk Record Office, MF 1496/4 (the school log of Bergh Apton), under 1 May 1884.
8. Mrs Hugh Bell, *At the Works: a Study of a Manufacturing Town* (London, 1907), p. 96.
9. G. Acorn, *One of the Multitude*, with an introduction by A. C. Benson (London, 1911), pp. 2, 4, 12, and 64. George's father was a drunkard.
10. J. C. Woollan, 'Table land in London', in *Living London*, ed. G. R. Sims, 3 vols (London, 1902–3), I, pp. 297–303, at pp. 298–9.
11. Ian Buxton, *The Enduring Legacy of Dewar's: A Company History* (Glasgow, 2009), pp. 34, 38, 39.
12. M. E. Bodiam, *A Short History of Guston* (Guston, 1975), pp. 11–12.
13. D. J. Oddy, *From Plain Fare to Fusion Food: British Diet from the 1890s to the 1990s* (Woodbridge, 2003), p. 74
14. P. Hadley, *The History of Bovril Advertising* (London, 1970), pp. 31, 33.

2. A Postman's Rubbish in Shropshire

THE Old Post Office, at Marshbrook in Shropshire, overlooks fields at the bottom of a lane which winds uphill through Castlehill Wood, towards the village of Acton Scott. Only a short walk from the station, it was well placed to receive supplies from Church Stretton and Shrewsbury, and to deliver mail in the neighbouring parishes of Acton Scott and Marshbrook. Two properties nestle together at the bottom of the lane: the post office itself and a smallholding to the rear. Owned and maintained for many years by the Actons of Acton Scott, both cottages are now in private hands. A Mr and Mrs Hayward were tenants there in the late nineteenth century. Mr Hayward had been the butler at the Hall for many years. In 1891, his widow Ann Hayward, then aged 77, held the tenement as 'Grocer and Postmistress'. Despite the title, she could not read or write, and her daughter, Mrs Bird, did the work for her.[1] Mrs Bird lived next door in the smallholding with her husband George, a farmer. After Mrs Hayward died, in the early 1890s, the Birds took over both tenements. In 1901, Mary Bird was Postmistress and George was listed as 'Sub Postmaster and Farmer'. He died early in 1910, and the Actons re-housed his widow in the Old School House, nearer the Hall in Acton Scott. Today the building houses the restaurant and tearooms of the Historic Working Farm. In 1910, somebody was needed to run the post office, so James Goddard of Oakwood Cottage, up the lane, was drafted in as 'Auxiliary Postman'. In 1911, he was 25 years old and married, with a family. Ten years earlier, he was identified in the census as a labourer at the mineral water works in Church Stretton, so he must have been familiar with the kind of machinery that was operated by James Goffe's heirs at the factory in Birmingham. By 1912, tenants had been found for the vacant properties, so Goddard returned to his farm. A station porter named Mr Phillips took on the post office at £2 10s per half year, and John Goodman paid £7 15s, per half year, for the smallholding. They remained in their cottages over the next two decades.[2]

Tenancy of the post office came with a pigsty and chicken run bordering the lane on the other side across from the back door. These appear on the

Figure 30. The Old Post Office, Marshbrook, c. 1910. The pigsty is visible on the other side of the lane, with the hedge behind, which screened the tipping ground.

Ordnance Survey of 1903.[3] Up behind the pigsty was a hedge, which can be seen in the early photograph (Fig. 30). It bounded the wood and the lane, aligned to the sty. Phillips the postmaster and station porter tipped his rubbish over the hedge behind the pigsty. Decades later, after the hedge had disappeared and the structure had been demolished, bottles, jars, and other items began washing out of the side of the steep earthen bank where years of hillwash ran down, now unimpeded. I noticed them in passing, in December 2011, and began work the following spring under the kind permission of Mr Rupert Acton. The first step was to clear some of the undergrowth, which concealed something like a wall of earth, rather like the side of a trench. Over the years, earth and rubbish had piled up behind the sty. Later, the stones of the rear wall were removed, leaving this vertical section showing the different layers of tipping in profile. I tidied it up with a trowel. At the bottom was a light clayey layer containing brick rubble, crockery and glass, and a few intact bottles all from the late Victorian era. It included part of a pot lid for Cleaver's 'genuine bear's grease', a dressing for the hair which cost sixpence and was made with imported bear's fat by F. S. Cleaver of Holborn. Above it was a darker layer containing ash, rusty tins, whole bottles and jars, crockery, and buckets of rubbish. This crusty layer dated from the early 1910s. Over this was an indistinct sequence of deposits from the 1910s and 1920s. Most of the rubbish could therefore be linked to Mr Phillips, being across the lane from his kitchen door, but the clayey layer evidently pre-dated his arrival.

Pigsties were a convenient place for rubbish (provided it was kept away from the area where the pigs rooted around), because the piggy smell could serve a purpose in disguising the odour of waste. Tipping near a pigsty could also reduce the number of journeys. Organic waste in one bucket could be fed to the pigs. Bottles and tins, in another, could be thrown over the hedge behind. The lowest layer, that clayey layer, contained house and garden rubbish. Bricks and window glass abounded; bottles and crockery were comparatively rare. Whatever this layer represented, it was surely an occasional tipping ground rather than the place where most of the household refuse was dumped. Broken dark-glass utility bottles for wine, beer, and vinegar turned up with intact inkwell-bottles of glass and stoneware. The utility bottles dated from the mid nineteenth century or earlier in some cases and had evidently been re-used. The inks, of the 1890s or 1900s, were the disposable kind, which we noted at Guston. It was no surprise to find inks at a post office. But who jettisoned them? There was no sign in the clayey layer of the clear-out operations that must have occurred after Mrs Bird finally left. Rather, this was probably one of several convenient locations where occupants occasionally tipped rubbish. When a new tenant came, the pattern changed. For a little while, at least, in the early 1910s, Phillips used this patch for much of his household waste, forming a crusty, wedge-shaped layer of buckets, tins, and bottles, lying thickest near the bottom of the slope, up behind the hedge.

Let's start by delving into a typical bucket of rubbish, visible in the photograph (Fig. 31). The sides are largely rusted away, but the sturdier base and ghostly outline of the bucket remain in the soil. Part of the rusty shell was removed before the photo was taken, to expose the contents in situ. Near the top is a small, bluish, rectangular bottle for Kutnow's powder, a popular laxative and cure-all. Beneath it is a standard white ceramic pudding bowl containing a decayed tin, over the remnants of a saucer, decorated with a transfer-printed blue floral pattern. The green beer bottle also in the bucket was sold by W. and H. E. Tanner of Shrewsbury. It is intact, but the neck lies hidden beneath another bit of the broken pudding bowl. All the bottles in the bucket were finished by hand: that is, none had been made in an automatic bottling machine. Nearby were the contents of a second bucket (Fig. 32), including a small, cylindrical bottle, which once contained 'Furniture Cream', made by the Stephenson brothers. It is lying on a larger, rectangular bottle,

Figure 31. The bottom of a rusted bucket. An upturned saucer, pudding bowl, and (inside the latter) a rusted tin made up some of its contents, with the green beer or wine bottle and (top left, base protruding) a bottle for Kutnow's Powder. Top left, outside the bucket: an early machine-made bottle from the Shrewsbury and Wem Brewery Co Ltd.

Figure 32. Part of the contents of a bucket. Top: the Stephensons' furniture cream. Middle: Eno's Fruit Salts. Bottom: a green half-pint beer from Walter T. Southam, Shrewsbury. Protruding to the right is the bottom of a broken stoneware bottle for seltzer water, imported from Passau in Bavaria.

of aqua glass, for 'Eno's Fruit Salts' – a bottle also found in the second pit at Guston. Below is a green half-pint beer from Walter T. Southam of Shrewsbury. In the early 1900s the Stephenson brothers were still selling cream in stoneware bottles. The contents of both buckets dated from the early 1910s. Above the first bucket, to the left but not inside, is an early green machine-made beer from the 'Shrewsbury and Wem Brewery Co Ltd', datable to the 1910s. We can take these buckets' contents as a snapshot of different categories of waste dumped behind the pigsty. The furniture cream bottle can stand for housekeeping products, while the pudding bowl represents food waste. The beers and saucer tell of drinking habits, and the 'Fruit Salts' and Kutnow's bottle stand for refuse associated with health concerns. Almost all the rubbish in the crusty layer divides into those categories.

Housekeeping waste was prominent in this layer. Someone had been doing a lot of scrubbing. Four bottles of the Stephenson brothers' cream had been thrown away intact. One was a large-sized specimen; the others were standard-size and must have held about as much cream as the stoneware bottles which glass superseded about the year 1910. Wide-mouthed vessels such as these were easier to manufacture in bottle machines than their narrow-necked counterparts, and suitable machinery was already available in the 1900s. Even so, and despite the fact that all four bottles were made at different glassworks, all were hand-finished. A rectangular bottle contained furniture cream too, perhaps supplied by the rival maker Adams, who sold his cream in bottles identical to this one. Whitish stains inside matched the white sludge in Stephensons' bottles (Fig. 33). It too was hand-finished. Half a dozen tins for Brasso also pointed to scrubbing. Brasso appeared in 1905, and the brand name could still be seen on two of the tins against its red and white background. Several tubular tins with perforated tops once contained scouring powder, for doorsteps, stoves, or cutlery; but the credentials of the brands they had promoted were no longer visible. No glut of cleaning products emerged in the upper layers. Going back to the occupants, now, we should remember that old Mrs Bird left the post office in 1910, after her husband died. The couple had lived there for decades into their old age, and there may have been quite an operation when their successor moved in. Edwardian post offices usually had wooden counters and hatches with a range of brass fittings. Given the date of the crusty layer, the early 1910s, it is reasonable to associate the furniture cream and Brasso with clean-up jobs in the years 1910–12 to restore the post office to its splendour. Yet it should be noted that Mr Phillips was a postmaster and a station porter, a man who spent no little time polishing

Figure 33. Top left: three bottles for Stephenson's furniture cream bottles, all hand-finished, early 1910s. Top right: ink bottles. Below, left to right: beer bottles for the firms of Tanner, Southam (× 2), Eadie, and Southam.

buttons on his uniforms and keeping his counter free of ink stains. He may have generated abnormal amounts of housekeeping waste.

One or more of the cottagers at Guston had worn military brass buttons. Had they shone them up on occasion and cleaned nothing else, a single bottle of Brasso in their household should have served for a few years. The refuse tipped in their garden in the 1900s did indeed contain a distinctive metal bottle of the kind used by Brasso and its competitors. Yet no such bottle turned up in their enormous pit of the 1910s, and not one furniture cream bottle was found in any of the Guston pits. The contrast between their housekeeping rubbish and that of their contemporary, Mr Phillips, could not be more striking. Either the labourers in Kent made their own furniture cream, or they scrubbed the kitchen table with soap and boiling water. No doubt their furniture was functional rather than the sort to be polished for display, so they generated almost no waste in the furniture and brass-polishing category.

Housekeeping refuse could also include bottles for blacking and blue. One or two of each, in stoneware, turned up in the 1900s pit at Guston, but bottles of this sort are less often dug up in later deposits, for, by about 1910, blacking was sold in tins and blue was sold in cubes, sometimes wrapped in muslin or cloth. Reckitt's was the most famous brand of 'bag blue' (Fig. 7). The fact that there were no bottles for blacking or blue in the layers of refuse at Marshbrook and the Guston rubbish from the 1910s is not therefore proof that these substances were not used. Still, it is clear that cleaning at the post office was reliant upon products sold in disposable packaging. Not only did our postmaster have the income to afford them, he may have attached greater importance to cleaning. There was evidence for this in an upper layer of rubbish, in the form of part of the copper tube of an early vacuum cleaner – a labour-saving machine, appearing in the 1900s. Adverts tempted middle-class housewives to invest in the expensive appliances by suggesting them as a means for dispensing with the maid. Cartoons of glum maids packing their carpet bags or clutching the redundant dustpan and brush appealed to employers who would rather do without their servants. The remnants of a vacuum cleaner in the rubbish dumped by Phillips illustrate his commitment to cleaning.

Food generated less disposable packaging than it does today. For much of its life the post office in Marshbrook doubled as the village store, receiving delivery of local produce and packaged groceries by rail. Butter arrived in large slabs, which were cut up for customers. Sugar came in big hessian sacks and was weighed up in blue paper bags. Treacle was poured from large barrels into jugs, basins, bowls, or into jars and tins provided by shoppers. When my grandmother was a little girl in the early 1920s she collected jam jars from the village dump at Tillingham, in Essex. The jars would be used for bringing home treacle, or re-filling with jam and preserves, or collecting frogspawn. Mr Phillips at the post office discarded usable jars which children would have wanted, including several stoneware ones for Hartley's jams. With a lighthouse trademark and factories in London and Liverpool, Hartley's were a very well known brand. The jars were not intrinsically disposable, in the way Bovril bottles were, but packaged jams were becoming more affordable. In 1901, a 3lb jar of jam, priced 7½d, provided more than a week's supply for a working family.[4] Jam was a staple, so households easily accrued a glut of the jars. Mr Phillips threw away transfer-printed ceramic jars for Keiller's 'Dundee Marmalade', although he may have re-used them first. There was also a large glass jar for bottled fruit, embossed 'T. W. Beach, Fruit Grower'. It had travelled to Shropshire from Brentwood in Essex, on the far side of

Figure 34. Base of a patent preserves jar, showing wear.

the kingdom where the heirs of Thomas Beach ran a successful concern. In 1910–11, when Bovril supplied Scott's expedition to the South Pole, Beach also won national prestige by supplying the jam. Within a few years, one of their jars was thrown with the rubbish at Marshbrook.

Households that bottled their own preserves in patent jars had less need to hoard the disposable variety. No such luxury as a patent jar surfaced at Guston, but several ended up behind the postman's pigs. One had the word 'PATENT' embossed on the base. It would have been sealed with a rubber ring and patent clamp-on lid. Damage to one of those components might explain why the jar was thrown away intact. If we turn this jar over to examine its base we see a rough ring of tiny scuffs and scratches, resulting from contact with hard surfaces (Fig. 34). Marks such as these show that the jar was re-used. As we might expect, the patent jar speaks of a long working life. Two other jars in the clear glass favoured by patent manufacturers had external screw threads at the top, for screw-on metal caps. One is hand-made; the other is machine-made. These too were patent jars, although of a cheaper kind. Larger preserves jars, with screw-on caps and a green-blue tinge, were made very cheaply in Belgium and imported. Fragments of three were excavated, but none whole (Fig. 35). In the third edition of his handbook *Fruit Bottling*

Figure 35. Neck and shoulders of a Belgian preserves jar.

(1916), Reverend W. Wilks had to modify his approach in light of attacks on allied shipping and war on the Western Front. 'Recent events', he observed, 'have restricted the importation of the cheap green-glass bottles which were so largely manufactured in Belgium'.[5] He went on to note that English bottles had since taken over on this front – and that these were superior, if a bit more expensive. The back cover of the reverend's book advertised 'Fowler's Patent Valve Vacuum Glass-Stoppered Jars', which should be purchased from Fowler of Reading at three shillings a dozen. The postman might just have afforded the capital outlay if his stock of Belgian jars had been depleted (as the casualties in his rubbish indicate). But 'Fowler's Complete Bottling Outfit', which had everything anyone needed, was probably out of his price range. At twenty shillings, the outfit would have cost more than two months' rent. Even the reverend author, despite the advert in his handbook, discouraged readers from investing in patent glassware, in such straitened times. No doubt they had a few old jars sitting around, so they should resort to the old method 'handed down from mother to daughter', of sealing those with a 'tie-down bladder, parchment top, or cork stopper'.[6] Wartime economy demanded re-use.[7]

In Marshbrook and other rural areas, milk and cream were fetched in jugs from a store or neighbouring farms, unless the dairy in question happened to sell its cream in cardboard cartons. Mostly, these were waste-free transactions, but occasionally cream was sold in cylindrical or vase-like jars – especially when it was sent by rail or sold in high-class outlets – and these found their way into the ground. Four or five, whole and broken, turned up at Guston. At Marshbrook, two appeared, both smashed before they were discarded. These were typical examples, plain with brown glaze. Other evidence of eating habits came in the form of a pressed glass cake stand, a jelly mould, and the usual white pudding bowls, all of which account for desserts universally eaten at that date. Bread, meat, and vegetables were invisible in the Marshbrook refuse, partly for the reason that organic matter rots and partly because the durable sort – chiefly bones – was fed to animals or crushed and used as fertiliser. The sauces, used to flavour what was otherwise plain fare, were advertised by lettering on their disposable containers. From the clayey layer at the bottom, a tall ornate bottle had contained either sauce or vinegar. From the crusty layer, a flattish bottle with reddish stains matched one from Guston, for gravy browning. Later deposits from the 1910s–20s contained more sauce bottles, most of them for brands. One proclaimed 'The A1 Sauce, Brand and Co, Ld, Mayfair'. There was an early bottle for 'Heinz Tomato Ketchup' too, the kind taken on the Scott expedition and still preserved in Scott's Hut, on Ross Island, Antarctica. Two were for 'Leckenby's KKK Sauce'. Another, with its stopper, bore the lettering 'Carton's HP Sauce' (not to be confused with 'Garton's HP Sauce'). A pair of aqua-glass, unembossed sauce bottles were identical to bottles used by Lea & Perrins and Goodall-Backhouse. Unlike the 'PATENT' jar, which was made in an early machine of unknown provenance, both had distinctive suction scars on the base, showing that they had been made in an Owens machine. All the bottles in the clayey layer and the vast majority in the crusty layer were hand-finished. Yet improved technology left a mark in this later assemblage of bottles. Those for Leckenby's sauce were machine-made, but they had been blown in a machine designed by one of Owens' rivals. The race was on to make disposable sauce bottles as cheaply as possible.

Tea was thought to maintain the health and strength of the body in equal degree as a substitute for food. 'Tea, therefore, saves food – stands to a certain extent in the place of food – while at the same time it soothes the body and enlivens the mind.' To the poor, claimed the author of *Facts and Hints*, 'tea is virtually tissue, and makes a supply of food'.[8] In North Yorkshire in the 1900s, tea was a crucial part of the diet. Mostly Indian tea, it retailed at 1s to 1s 4d a pound and was bought in small packets containing an ounce, which sold for 1d.[9] In London, at that date, a workman's wife could purchase a quarter of a pound of tea from the grocers for 4½d. With care, this would last her family a week unless a friend came to tea whereupon a second ounce was needed. The leaves could be re-used for a second and third brew. A quarter of a pound of ready ground coffee cost 3d; but workers preferred the taste of coffee with chicory, which strengthened the flavour.[10] Bottles for extract of coffee with chicory were found in the 1900s rubbish at Guston. Broken teapots and teacups always turn up in old tips, and Marshbrook was no different. Some of the cups and saucers were decorated in blue, grey, or red; some were plain white and appeared to be a cheaper sort. The same distinction was apparent in the crockery in the pit from the 1910s at Guston. It is known that decorated cups were reserved for Sunday afternoon tea and visitors, while plain ones served for everyday use. Retailers' catalogues of the time advertised decorated ware for the dining room and bedroom, and plain white pieces for servants and for use in the kitchen.[11] Neither Marshbrook nor Guston contained the bottles that would prove that bottled tea and coffee were popular during the war. We saw that the labourers at Guston turned to Bovril in large quantities, but only a single Bovril bottle was found at Marshbrook. The solitary bottle for Foster Clark's 'Eiffel Tower Lemonade' told a similar story: that a drink enjoyed at Guston was no comfort to the postmaster. Both brands certainly reached the Shropshire post office, but neither impressed Phillips, who favoured a stronger brew.

The Shropshire Brewery Company Ltd was registered in 1898 and, shortly after that, changed its name to the Shrewsbury and Wem Brewery Company Ltd. For the first decade or so, the firm bottled its beer in golden-amber, hand-finished, half-pint bottles, sealed with corks and embossed with its name. When its glassworks started using automated bottle machines, about 1910, a different mix of ingredients came in for making the glass: for the mix had to be compatible with the specifications of the mechanised process. From then on the bottles came out emerald green with a hint of turquoise (Fig. 36). As to the design, shape, and embossing, they remained the same. The machine-made bottles, however, had a seam running through the lip. This was a subtle revolution in the life of a beery postmaster. Mr Phillips discarded such bottles copiously. Three of the amber ones and six of the green machine-made ones turned up, intact. More than a dozen broken specimens also surfaced – many of which must have broken in the ground judging by the fractures and the presence of all the pieces. Wear patterns on the bases of the three hand-made bottles revealed heavier use than corresponding wear on the machine-made ones. Evidently the older bottles had been refilled many times, the newer bottles less so. All appeared in the crusty layer, of the early 1910s. The wastage of these re-usable bottles in this instance would have been exacerbated by Marshbrook's relative isolation. In Shrewsbury they could have been returned to the brewery, pubs, or stores. Outside their zone of re-use, however, these empties were redundant. Neither Mr Phillips nor any

Figure 36. Bottles from Shrewsbury and Wem Brewery Company Ltd. Left: two amber bottles, 1898–c. 1910. Right: an emerald/turquoise machine-made bottle.

local child rootling through his rubbish would go all the way to the nearest town to collect a meagre deposit. And it was hardly worth going with half-pint bottles to fetch a supply of beer, when sturdy demijohns – and fragments of these were found – made the process simple and easy. In any case, mass production created a surplus of these bottles, so more than twenty from the Shrewsbury and Wem brewery ended up behind the sty.

Other beer bottles suffered the same redundancy. The example photographed in the bucket (Fig. 31) was a hand-made one from W. and H. E. Tanner in Shrewsbury. Another from the same firm said 'W. & H. E. Tanner, Welshpool', whence it might have travelled via the brewery in Shrewsbury, like its counterpart.

Two green beers, also of half-pint capacity, were embossed 'Walter T. Southam, Old Salop Brewery, Shrewsbury'. A later example had the name 'Thomas Southam and Sons Ltd, Wyle Cop, Shrewsbury'. The Southams are listed separately in the 1913 directory. Some bottles came from farther afield. Three pint-sized specimens displayed the pictorial trademark of 'Whitbread & Co, Ltd, London'. Another came from 'Truman and Co, Ltd, London and Burton'. An aqua, hand-made beer proclaimed 'James Eadie, Ltd, Burton on Trent'. On the rear was the command 'For owner's exclusive use, return forthwith when empty'. Extensive wear to its base revealed that this bottle, the only one of its kind, had been used a lot, not necessarily by James Eadie (Fig. 33). All in all, over thirty beer bottles had been discarded intact. Five came from London and Burton on Trent; the rest came from Shrewsbury. Brands had clearly not broken in upon this market. Local breweries supplied the postman's ale. The author of *Facts and Hints* says, 'To those whose diet is poor or insufficient ale is very nutritious'.[12] There is no reason to think that the postman's diet was poor.[13] He simply liked his beer. At that date, mild ale was favoured by the working classes and retailed at the price of 4d a quart, or 2d pint (rising to 2½d in 1914.) An ordinary working man spent up to a third of his income on beer and tobacco, giving the rest to his wife.[14] Phillips jettisoned enough intact bottles behind that pigsty to hold thirteen pints of beer, which is not very much – maybe only a few days' moderately heavy swilling. The possibility remains, therefore, that only a few surplus bottles were thrown out. The majority may have been re-used.

The only bottle of the kind with a marble in its neck, for carbonated beverages, bore the name of the Shrewsbury and Wem Brewery Company, Ltd (Fig. 37). It was discarded intact at a time when bottles of this design were fast disappearing, because they had to be made by hand. Mineral waters, to the author of *Facts and Hints*, were 'all natural waters which have been found useful in the treatment of disease'. Each was famed for its particular curative properties. At Carlsbad, Neiderselters, Buxton, and similar spas, invalids visited the baths and took the water. 'Seltzer' was a 'highly carbonated alkaline water' which 'raises the spirits and promotes digestion.' As the author of *Facts and Hints* explains, 'Seltzer [Selters] is a small town of the lower Rhine in Germany; its water is transported in stone bottles, well corked, to almost every part of Europe'. Seltzer was very highly recommended for combatting night sweats and fevers.[15] A bottle pulled from the Thames and another found at Guston came to our attention earlier. A third surfaced under the crusty layer at Marshbrook. The front was incised 'Ober-Selters, Nassau', around the German eagle. Apart from this foreign relative, all the mineral waters in Marshbrook were from nearby

Figure 37. Centre: the only 'Codd bottle' from Marshbrook, early 1910s, named after the inventor Hiram Codd, who patented the design in the 1870s.

Church Stretton (Fig. 38). Church Stretton grew up during the late Victorian era around a mineral spa in the hills. Nestling in the valley under a pre-Cambrian outcrop known as Long Mynd, which is occasionally capped with snow, the resort gained the nickname 'Little Switzerland'. The manufacturing industry there and the main employer was the Stretton Hills Mineral Water Works, which added CO_2 to the local water and bottled it for sale. James Goddard worked there in his teenage years, around 1901. He bottled water not only in the egg-shaped bottles patented by William Hamilton but also in the flat-bottomed version, based on the same design. The point of Hamilton's bottles, of course, was to force retailers to store them on their side. Flat-bottomed ones defeated this purpose, though, presumably, they reminded purveyors of an appropriate manner of storage without inconveniencing customers. Three of these bottles turned up, intact, in the crusty layer of the early 1910s. Fragments of others were found scattered upon the hillside, and all were embossed with the name of the local firm. Minor wear to the bases revealed some re-use before the bottles were discarded in a usable condition.

Figure 38. Left: a flat-bottomed 'Hamilton' bottle from the Stretton Hills Mineral Water Co., Ltd. Right: a stoneware bottle from Niederselters, 1866–80 (thrown into the Thames near London Bridge).

Mineral water was as much a remedy as a beverage, useful in combating stomach upsets and warding off night fevers. Illnesses were ascribed to impurities of the blood, excessive bile, and dietary imbalance. Doctors were rare in old rural England. Only in the direst event, and at great expense, would people call the doctor. Common ailments had common remedies. Treacle, to give one example, was a popular blood purifier – a springtime 'ablutent'. Occasionally, the tenants of the post office invested in prepared medicines. 'Bad lungs' gave rise to coughing and shortness of breath, but a prominent branded remedy, 'Owbridge's Lung Tonic', claimed to strengthen them and reduce ill effects. It was sold in bottles of four sizes, the cheapest priced at 1s 1½d (the one and a half pence covering the stamp duty, which was levied on proprietary medicines). On opening the packet, the sufferer found a pamphlet explaining that cough lozenges and homely cures were

Figure 39. Top, left to right: Leckenby's KKK Sauce; Kutnow's Powder (×2); patent preserves jar. Centre: inks. Below, left to right: Stretton Hills Mineral Water Co., Ltd; Dr Adolf Hommel's Haematogen; Owbridge's Lung Tonic, and a patent preserves jar. Bottom: bottle stoppers.

insufficient, and that linseed poultices would make a cough worse. 'Kay's Linseed Compound' was a rival of Owbridge's in the patent medicine trade. If the patient persists, the pamphlet concluded, 'cure is quite certain'. The postman paid quite a sum to prove the point. Although the paper packets and pamphlets had rotted in the ground, three large Owbridge's bottles, each of 6½ fluid ounces capacity, each of which would have cost two shillings and ninepence, surfaced in the rubbish. They dated from roughly the time (1909) when the British Medical Association, dismayed by the proliferation of bogus cures, published their exposé of 'secret remedies', after subjecting samples to analysis. Owbridge's contained a tiny and relatively worthless quantity of a couple of active ingredients. The remainder was mostly honey and oils of aniseed and peppermint (Fig. 39).[16]

Another pricey and doubtful remedy consumed by the postmaster was 'Dr

*Figure 40. Dr Adolf
Hommel's Haematogen
emerges from the
ground.*

Adolf Hommel's Haematogen', a blood tonic (Fig. 40). Costing an immense four shillings a bottle, it was for dire cases. Such remedies may have been sold at the post office, and certainly in Church Stretton. Nine empty bottles for 'Kutnow's Powder', five of them intact, suggest that one remedy became habitual (Fig. 41). Early adverts for Kutnow's promoted it as a cure-all rather than a 'specific' suitable for one particular ailment. A postman could have taken it for headaches, indigestion, biliousness, constipation, gout, diabetes, or all of the above – on a bad day. An advert from 1898 declared, somewhat carefully, 'we are informed that Kutnow's Powder has been prescribed for His Royal Highness the Prince of Wales' (Fig. 42). It also says that the effervescent powder was made from the (evaporated) waters of the famous European Mineral Springs, without stating which springs contributed. The name Kutnow did sound like it should belong to a learned medical man, resident somewhere within Bohemia and convinced of his product's scientific credentials. 'Eno's Fruit Salts' was another ablutent uncovered at Marshbrook (Fig. 32). Eno's salt, 'Veno's Lightning Cough Cure', and 'Dinnerford's Magnesia', for stomach upsets, had all surfaced at Guston and evidently sold here as well. Layers of waste from the later 1910s contained jars for Pond's creams, for piles and the like, embossed with Pond's name, and a variety from Boot's 'Regesan' range for Toilet Cream and Regesan Morning Powder (Fig. 43). These novel toiletries were sold in elaborately moulded green glass with embossed metal screw-on lids, and they were reaching an expanding market because Jesse Boot sold his compounds cheaply, undercutting other druggists.

Figure 41 (right). Kutnow's Powder, from Marshbrook.

Figure 42 (below). An advert for Kutnow's Powder, suggesting royal patronage. 1898.

Have you tried

KUTNOW'S
Improved Effervescent Powder

when you have headache, pains in different parts of the body and feel tired and languid and depressed?

It is made from the waters of the famous European Mineral Springs noted for diseases of the Liver and Stomach and always relieves such symptoms and cures

Indigestion	Sluggish Liver	Biliousness
Constipation	Dyspepsia	Gout
Catarrh of the Stomach		Diabetes

Samples sent free and postpaid to every applicant mentioning McClure's. Positively refuse substitutes ; they are worthless. Price $1.00 per bottle postpaid. Sold by all reliable druggists! Should, however, your druggist not keep it, apply direct to

KUTNOW BROS., 13 ASTOR PLACE (Mercantile Library Building), NEW YORK CITY.

" This is very strongly recommended," says "London Land and Water," "by many acknowledged medical authorities, for use by sufferers from rheumatism, gout and disorders of the stomach, liver and kidneys. It is also highly spoken of as a corrective medicine most suitable for people leading sedentary lives. We are informed that Kutnow's Improved Effervescent Powder has been prescribed for His Royal Highness the Prince of Wales and other members of the Royal Family, which affords an indication of the opinion of the remedy entertained by the medical profession."

ASTHMA, BRONCHITIS, GRIP AND KINDRED TROUBLES.
Sufferers from these ailments should try either **Kutnow's Anti-Asthmatic Powder** or **Cigarettes**, which are employed under the highest medical authority for Asthma, Bronchitis, Catarrh, Influenza, and ordinary Colds. To obtain Free and Postpaid Samples write for either the **Anti-Asthmatic Powder** or for the **Cigarettes**, and mention McClure's.

Figure 43. Regesan Toilet Cream. c. 1915–20.   *Figure 44. Germolene tin, from Marshbrook. 1920s.*

At Guston and Marshbrook, we see mirrored the rise of the retailing chemists in the proliferation of their packaging.

While I dug, a giant bathtub hung suspended in the section of my trench. It was the round sort, with a flared pouring lip for tipping out bathwater. The bather had to squat like a toad or stand with a washstand jug and pour water over his back, unless he had an assistant, as young children did. In very cold weather Phillips might have got out of bed to find a crust of ice on the water. Eventually, he filled the bath with rubbish and dumped it behind the pigsty. It hung there protruding from my section, overlying the crusty layer and deposits of the later 1910s. Trowelling away inside, I found rubble, paste jars, and green poison bottles, which dated its final service as a receptacle for rubbish to the 1920s. In with it all was a stoneware bottle, for ginger beer, discarded after it had split neatly in two (Fig. 45). The split called to mind the breaks that occur when fermenting homemade brews are left too long in bottles, or when bottles are left outdoors and exposed to freeze-thaw action. But only one half was present, so the bottle had not broken in the ground. Nor was it the sort of bottle Mr Phillips discarded intact. Like my grandfather Arthur (1908–78), he would have kept such bottles in his shed, for brewing beer, discarding those that exploded. This specimen bore the stamp of the Belper & Denby pottery in Derbyshire and the 'EX' stamp for the excise tax on stone bottles, which was levied between 1817 and 1834 (Fig. 46). There

Figure 45 (above). Left: a stoneware bottle from the Belper & Denby potteries, found in the rubbish at Marshbrook. 1817–34. Centre: for comparison, a bottle made at the Denby and Codnor Park potteries, where the company re-located. 1834–c. 1850. Right: a bottle made at the Denby pottery after 1850. The vitreous stoneware bottles remained largely unchanged throughout the nineteenth century.

Figure 46 (right). The EX 5 stamp on the Belper & Denby bottle.

was a number 5 after the 'EX', which may relate to the rate of duty (at five shillings per hundredweight), or bear some other significance. Either way, the bottle was a hundred years old when discarded; and such finds are by no

Figure 47. A selection of items discarded at Marshbrook.

means uncommon. Arthur in the 1970s was making wine in stone flagons that were about one hundred years old.

Although three stone inkwell-bottles and a pouring ink turned up in the clayey layer, there were no intact stone bottles in the layers from the 1910s. As we saw at Guston, utilitarian stoneware was largely disappearing by 1910, save for a few late furniture creams and master inks that often taper inwards a little at the base. Ginger beer bottles were the exception, because glass ones risked exploding; and, because they were durable and serviceable, country folk kept them. The typical mix of lamp flues and globes, flower pots, mixing bowls and pans, along with a hot water kettle and a teaspoon thrown out by mistake, accounts for the rest of the waste discarded over the hedge behind the pigsty. Further dumping took place along the edge of the track leading from the sty to the woods, where larger items, including fittings from someone's kitchen range, were carted away from the tenements and tipped on land belonging to the lords of that neighbourhood, the Actons of Acton Scott. A mix of packaging recovered from behind the sty is arranged in Figure 47.

Notes

1. Notes made by a great aunt of Mr Rupert Acton, cited with his kind permission.
2. Shropshire County Archives, Shrewsbury Record Office, 2536/18: The Acton Scott Estate, Rental books, No. 67 onwards.
3. Shropshire 64.1, 2nd edition, 1903.
4. Arthur Morrison, 'Family budgets. 1. A workman's budget', *Cornhill Magazine* 10 (April, 1901), pp. 446–56.
5. W. Wilks, *Fruit Bottling*, 3rd edition (1916), p. 3.
6. *Ibid.*, pp. 3, 1.
7. On the importance of salvage during World War I, see T. Cooper, 'Challenging the 'refuse revolution': war, waste, and the rediscovery of recycling, 1900–50', *Historical Research* 81, no. 214 (2008), pp. 710–31.
8. *Facts and Hints*, p. 373.
9. Bell, *At the Works*, p. 97.
10. Morrison, 'A workman's budget'.
11. For example, Pellatt & Co, *Catalogue of Glass and Earthenware* (London, 1870), p. 24.
12. *Facts and Hints*, p. 12.
13. Unless he actually consumed furniture cream and drank Brasso.
14. Charles Booth, (notebook) B349, p. 55: http://booth.lse.ac.uk/notebooks/b349/jpg/55.html.
15. *Facts and Hints*, pp. 272–5.
16. *Secret Remedies: What they Cost and What they Contain*, based on analyses made for the British Medical Association (London, 1909), pp. 13–14.

3. A Norfolk Rectory

IN her book *Waste and Want: a Social History of Trash*, Susan Strasser observes that 'sorting is an issue of class'. 'The wealthy', she says, 'can afford to be wasteful', whereas the poor 'waste less to begin with, and they scavenge for materials to use or sell.'[1] We saw earlier that the rich inhabitants of Kensington and Chelsea discarded more glass containers than the poorer residents of St Pancras; by the 1910s however, packaging had become so cheap to manufacture that our labourers in Guston wasted glass in comparable amounts. A household of labourers living in Well Cottages may have earned less than £40 a year. The rural postman Mr Phillips may have earned in the region of £60–70 a year, with £5 p/a on rent. A rector in a comfortable benefice gathered an annual income of £500, rent-free. Would this affluence have turned him into a wasteful man, as Susan Strasser suggests?

Hempstead is a village a little north of Hickling in the expansive fertile farmland north of the Norfolk Broads. Today it would take the better part of four hours to drive from Hempstead to Marshbrook and roughly the same from either location to Guston. Coming into Hempstead from Stalham the traveller turns left from the main road up a driveway arranged to present a prospect of the rectory. This is a Georgian building of well-finished brick, extended in Victorian times, and fronted by a lawn (Fig. 48). The rectory, annexed to nearby Lessingham, was in the gift of King's College, Cambridge, with a gross yearly value of £500, deriving from tithe income and 70 acres of glebe.[2] Grade 1 soil (subsoil, sand, and clay) produced good crops of wheat, oats, and barley, with pasture for the poor. The rector from 1895 to 1904 was Reverend John Francis Kendall. Curiously, he was the son of a gardener, born in 1862 in Blackheath in Kent. His father later became Head Gardener at Weeting Hall in Norfolk – the residence of William Angerstein, a magistrate and landowner farming 2,500 acres. His farm and estate employed 57 men and 9 boys and over a dozen domestic servants. Angerstein's daughter Julia paid for the young John Kendall to study History at Cambridge. Then they ran off and married in Greenwich in 1886. Living in Cambridge, they registered the birth

Figure 48. Hempstead rectory, near Stalham, Norfolk. Photo: Ronnie Pestell.

of a son, Eric Angerstein K., in December 1887, after holidaying in Cromer that Easter. In 1888, they moved to Notting Hill, where Kendall became the curate of St Clement's. Dustmen carted their refuse to the Kensington dust-heap. In December 1889, they registered the birth of a daughter, Ruth. A second son, Locke, followed in December 1890, just as the family were moving to the Cotswalds twenty miles north of Oxford, where Kendall would became vicar of Great and Little Tew. Their second daughter Evelyn was born there in March 1895. Later that year, Kendall's connexion to King's procured the Hempstead living, when the rector, James Pounder Whitney, left. Again the family packed their bags. They were heading for the Norfolk coast.

Arriving at the rectory and heading up the drive, the Kendalls would have been greeted by a brick-built privy with a commodious cesspit (Fig. 49). No doubt it had been emptied before the family's arrival, but it could not have been long before the convenience began to fill and vapours wafted up the shaft to concentrate their fug. Earth closets were always temperamental, and Julia, with a new baby, would have worried about typhoid, a hazard in the 1890s. Flushing toilets could be plumbed in, and the rectory may already have had one. It was therefore decided that the cesspit should be filled and

Figure 49. The privy at the rectory. It is shown on a plan of the house from the 1820s. The cesspit has been partially filled in, but the arched top of the shaft can be seen in the photo. Behind is the pantry.

sealed. The mortared, brick-lined hole, four feet square and five feet deep, became a tip for rubbish which lay there undisturbed beneath a flowerbed, until a December day in 2012, when Ronnie and Jackie Pestell invited me to dig it a bit deeper than normal (Fig. 50). That day I knew nothing of the Kendalls. Ben, my muddy helper, assisted; and all we knew after a two-day dig was that we had on our hands a crate of salvaged bulbs and the contents of a rubbish pit from the 1890s. The latest datable objects in the pit were two Eiffel Tower Fruit Juice bottles, dating after the firm's foundation in 1891, and two identical saucers with a potter's mark dating after 1893.[3] From this, it was unclear whether the trash belonged to Whitney (rector from 1891 to 1895) or Kendall (1895–1904). After a bit of research, the fancy bisque doll's head, a child's bone toothbrush, and a bottle for Mellin's Infant Food resolved that question, because Whitney and his wife never had children, and it was unlikely that a doll of that quality, and the toothbrush, had belonged to the child of a resident servant (Fig. 51). The refuse belonged to the Kendalls. Moreover the Mellin's Food bottle lay at the very bottom of the pit, giving a likely date for when tipping began.

Figure 50. The outline of the pit comes into view, revealing some of its contents. On the left, the clay cap overlying the fill has yet to be removed.

Mellin's Food provided babies with pre-digested nutrients by converting starch into soluble glucose through the fermenting action of malt. Adverts from the 1890s presented a range of testimonials from middle class parents, claiming to have raised their children on Mellin's Food mixed with milk, from ages ranging between a mere six weeks and four months upwards. In the 1890s evidently, Mellin's Food was sold as a substitute for breast milk. A decade later, the company marketed this product to mothers who were weaning and those wishing to improve the diets of one-year-olds. Two heaped tablespoons dissolved in twelve tablespoons of water were to be mixed with twenty tablespoons of good fresh milk.[4] The impressive baby, Lester R. Funk, pictured in a promotional booklet, gurgled in testimony to the nutritional quality of Mellin's Food. In the 1890s such a bottle must have cost the Kendalls two shillings, more than most could afford. Ironworkers' wives in the cottages of North Yorkshire could not afford fresh milk for their children, let alone Mellin's Food to mix with it. Mostly they purchased condensed milk in tins. If their children wanted nourishment or suffered sickness and diarrhoea, they might resort to buying a tumbler of brandy, but that was no guaranteed remedy.[5] At Hempstead, their nurse would

Figure 51. *Childhood at the rectory. A broken tile shows girls playing. Part of a tiny saucer, decorated in gold leaf, belonged to a pampered doll, as did the fragment of a fine bisque doll's head. They were Ruth or Evelyn's toys. The other item is a child's toothbrush, of bone.*

Figure 52. *Mellin's Infants' Food bottle, from the bottom of the pit. c. 1895.*

have given Mellin's food to Evelyn in her early months in 1895–6 and discarded the bottle into the privy at that time (Figs 52 and 53).

Tipping thus began probably in 1895, not long after the Kendalls moved in. A rich organic soil at the bottom of the pit, pungent with ammonia, showed that they used their privy for a short while before filling it. In this soil was a honey pot with about an inch of putty inside it. Lead flashing and broken window glass suggested repairs to the rectory when the family moved in. The pot had been re-used, to hold putty for fitting new windowpanes. After that, it had not been worth the trouble of extracting the putty to retain the pot, so it joined a mixture of crockery, bricks, tins, and bottles, together with a bucket or two full of refuse. We would have to imagine what it would take to fill four or five large wheelie bins, because the pit filled in by the Kendalls had roughly that capacity. Was filling the pit a priority – in which case did they hunt around for hardcore with a mind to filling it quickly – or did they let it fill at a natural pace? How

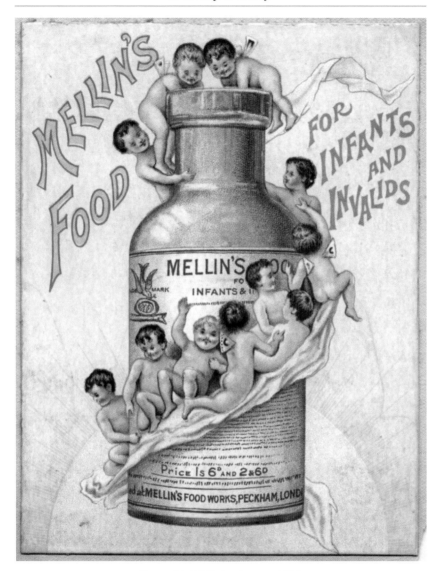

Figure 53. Mellin's advert. c. 1900.

long did it all take? Smashed crockery can give us clues, for it is possible to estimate how many items of crockery have been discarded in any tip by counting the bases of cups, bowls, plates, *etc.*, while allowing of course that a number of

Figure 54. 'Genevese' serving plates, by Thomas and Benjamin Godwin of Burslem, 1809–34. Discarded, c. 1895.

them will have fragmented and will need to be reassembled if an accurate figure is required. The privy contained between 90 and 120 items, excluding vessels sold as packaging, such as bottles and jars. We know, from the 1901 census, that the Kendall household at Hempstead consisted of three family members (John, Julia, and Evelyn), two servants (Anna and Emma, the cook and the housemaid aged 17 and 15 respectively), and two Cambridge undergraduates, boarding over the Easter vacation to study under Kendall. The three elder children, Eric, Ruth, and Locke, were then at boarding schools in Oxford, but in 1895 they were all under eight years old and must still have been living at home. At that date, there may also have been a third servant, the nursemaid, given that the Kendalls took on a nurse, as a third servant, in 1891, to nurse Ruth. In 1895 therefore their household consisted of two parents, four children, two or three servants, and occasional boarders. Applying our modest estimate, that a family of four might have broken 35 ceramic items a year, excluding packaging, we find that the Kendalls could have broken all the crockery in the privy in barely more than a year. This calculation, of course, is based on a rate of natural wastage, which does not allow for the clearing-out of unwanted items.

Figure 55. Coalport cups, 1881–91. Discarded, c. 1895. (A seventh was found after the photo was taken.)

Among the objects in the pit were eight or more broken serving plates bearing a blue transfer-printed pattern, labelled 'Genevese' (Fig. 54). Made between 1809 and 1834 by Thomas and Benjamin Godwin of Burslem, they were at least sixty years old when discarded and may have been cleared out of a cupboard either as the remnant of an old dinner service or as tatty pieces no longer suitable for table. Perhaps they were lurking in a corner, left by the previous rector. Seven Coalport cups, for cocoa or tea, may have been rejected too, though they were not nearly as old, dating between 1881 and 1891 (Fig. 55). But perhaps crockery left in cupboards had to make room for the Kendalls' own. Most of the items that were datable dated from the 1880s, hinting at an average shelf life of ten years. Typically two or three items of a kind were broken. There were two Minton plates, dating between 1873 and 1891; two small saucers by Baker and Co Ltd of Fenton, manufactured after 1893; three pieces from a washstand set, wearing the diamond registration mark for 1864; three smashed plates from the Yorkshire potters Samuel Barker & Sons, made between 1851 and 1893; two broken members from another washstand set, by Doulton, dating 1882–1891; two unmarked candlesticks, eggcups, *etc.* (Fig. 56).[6] Some items had certainly

Figure 56. Crockery from the privy. Discarded, c. 1895.

been dumped intact, among them a lidded ceramic sanitary bucket, which fractured in the privy shaft, and a jug with a chipped spout. The banded ware jug, capacity two quarts, and a Mocha ware bowl need not have ended their days as they did, for both were easy to repair even after further fragmentation in the hole (Fig. 57). *Facts and Hints for Everyday Life* had advice on how to mend crockery, but the Kendalls had no need to salvage a jug or bowl of the kind commonly loaned from a local pub. They also hired crockery for occasional

Figure 57. A Mocha ware bowl and quart jug, repaired by the author.

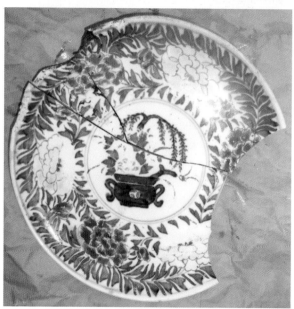

Figure 58. Most of a hand-painted oriental saucer.

parties, when guests added their breakages to the rubbish in the hole. More will be said on parties. In answer to the question, how long it took to fill their privy-pit, we might conclude not more than a year, 1895–6, and possibly less.

Most of the crockery came from the Staffordshire potteries, though there were also imported items such as a Chinese ginger jar, a Japanese enamelled saucer, and fine china from Limoges (Fig. 58). A plate by Haviland & Co was made at Limoges between 1879 and 1886. A host of hand-decorated

Figure 59. Pieces of china from Limoges, hand-painted tableware decorated in gold leaf, and part of a doll's saucer of matching quality.

items such as were not present at Guston or Marshbrook included white tableware patterned in gold leaf (Fig. 59). An income of £500 p/a could buy fine ceramics, native or shipped from afar. Fancy tiles were affordable. One displaying the King's College armorial crest may already have adorned the rectory. Another, transfer-printed brown, shows two girls playing above the word JANUARY. This was one of twelve designed by Helen Mills and made by Wedgwood in 1878, sold as 'The months'. Like the putty, these tiles may imply that the rectory was being re-decorated. There were vases for single flowers, one of them finely etched, and a moulded black-glass spill holder (to hold splints or tapers before the introduction of matches). Pressed-glass moulded drinking cups jostled with free-blown beakers in shades of green or turquoise (Figs 60 and 61). Chamber pots and other practical ceramics, such as mixing bowls and pudding bowls, were found at all three sites.

Figure 60. Beakers and other bits.

Figure 61. Cut glass beakers and dishes, a decanter neck, a black glass spill holder in the shape of a classical column, and two specimen vases missing their feet (far right).

79

*Figure 62. Two cups from
'J. G. Pike, Confectioner',
a caterer with shops in
Norwich.*

Shopping for tableware and other items became fashionable in the late Victorian era. In large towns and cities department stores appeared, which enticed middle class women with sumptuous displays, reading rooms, and refreshments for 'Five o' clock tea'. A keen observer in London remarked in 1903: 'There are pretty and artistically decorated tea rooms attached to high class chocolate and bon-bon shops to which elegantly dressed ladies repair for tea, coffee and cream, and ices.'[7] Shops of this sort, known as confectioners' shops, were also places wealthier shoppers took their children for lemonade or ginger beer. Julia Kendall would have come upon them in Norwich. Caley's, also the manufacturers, specialized in the sale of aërated waters, ginger beer, cocoa, and chocolates, which were sold in boxes with decorative frills. Like James Goffe, his contemporary in Birmingham, Mr Caley used silver-coated cylinders to ensure that no residues of copper contaminated the drinks. His adverts insisted that Caley's mineral waters were a favourite of the Prince and Princess of Wales, though they sold for no more than a penny a bottle. John Greaves Pike was another confectioner in Norwich, with shops in Red Lion Street and in Timberhill Street. Pike sold various beverages in cups emblazoned with his name, 'J. G. PIKE, CONFECTIONER', two of which ended up in the Kendalls' cesspit (Fig. 62). Had one been found alone we might have guessed that a child had taken it as a souvenir, but two looks less like childish theft. In the same corner of the pit, we excavated at least 23 bottles for powdered fruit juices, each of which was supposed to yield two gallons according to the advert from 1899. Together with the cups, so many bottles from one deposit hint that the Kendalls hired caterers and had a party at the rectory. We know that country clergy in Norfolk hired in provisions for garden parties from Norwich because the vicar of East Dereham and diarist,

Rev. Benjamin Armstrong, records a party thrown by his wife on 20 August 1884. Anticipating costs, he noted laconically: 'Ices and fruit were supplied from Norwich, for which, I suspect, there will be something to pay'.[8]

John Pike is listed in the census of 1891 as a confectioner and caterer, living in Norwich, with his wife Lydia, four daughters, and one general servant. In 1895, he was 46 years old. Guidance on hiring in caterers could be found in advice literature, such as *Party-Giving on Every Scale*, which included chapters on garden parties and children's parties. Touching the former, the anonymous author explains that 'ladies consider it incumbent on themselves to entertain their neighbours, once or twice in summer months'. Smaller parties drew 25–40 guests; typical gatherings averaged 40–100. Conventionally they ran from 4pm to 7pm, with refreshments served indoors or on tables outside, and rugs and chairs set out for seating. 'Indispensable' refreshments included tea, coffee, cake, biscuits, and claret cup, a drink made by mixing claret and soda water. Four bottles of claret and four of soda water provided a gallon, and half a gallon was considered adequate for 80 guests at tea. Desirable refreshments at garden parties included cold meat, ale, and sherry. Two women servants should pour out tea and coffee; another could serve strawberries and ices, while a manservant attended in the tea room to open bottles of soda and wine. Four gallons of coffee would do for 80 people at afternoon tea. Sporting entertainments demanded greater liquid refreshment. The author thought that the china cupboard of the house would furnish 2½ dozen cups and saucers, seldom enough. Additional cups and saucers could be hired for between 9d and 1s 6d per dozen. Tumblers and wine glasses cost a shilling per dozen to hire. Fifty children, at a party, required five-dozen cups and saucers, allowing some for the ladies that would accompany them, reckoning on 25–30 adults to every fifty children. The fare at children's parties included tea and cakes, fruit juices, and the like.[9] John Greaves Pike advertised his business on the crockery hired in by the Kendalls, though to how many guests and at what event no one now can reveal. In theory, 23 bottles of fizzy fruit crystals could have provided 46 gallons! In reality, surely, far less dilution occurred in preparing these drinks, given that five bottles came up in a single bucket in one of the Guston pits. At Hempstead we can envisage whole bottles being tipped into a steaming, sugary vat, as wasps buzzed around and children brought their cups.

The fruit juice bottles provide an interesting cross section of what was available in Norwich in 1895. Of twenty-three recovered, nineteen came from a Norwich firm, two from a firm in Bristol, and two from a firm in Kent. Thirteen were embossed 'D[E] CARLES, RIPE FRUIT DRINK, PRICE

Figure 63. Fruit juice bottles. Left to right: two of De Carle's, one of Foster Clark's, showing the Eiffel Tower, and one for 'Big Wheel Fruit Juices', Bristol. All c. 1895.

4$^{1/2D}$/ FOR MAKING FRUIT SYRUPS/ D^E CARLE & SON, NORWICH'; and six were embossed 'D^E CARLES RIPE FRUIT DRINKS/ THE ONLY ORIGINAL AND GENUINE/ FOR MAKING FRUIT SYRUPS/ D^E CARLE & SON, NORWICH'. Two others bore the following: 'BIG WHEEL/ FRUIT JUICES/ GILL & CO/ 45 WILDER ST/ BRISTOL'. Another two bore the name, 'FOSTER CLARK & C^O, MAIDSTONE/ EIFFEL TOWER FRUIT JUICES' with a pictorial trademark showing the Eiffel Tower embossed on the two remaining panels (Fig. 63). All bottles had burst-off lips and held the same capacity. The assemblage shows that in 1895 the local brand was still dominant, while others with aspirations were creeping in. The competitors, 'Big Wheel' and 'Eiffel Tower' fruit juices, advertised their wares with brand images hinting at leisure and tourism. The Bristol company at the mineral works at 45 Wilder Street later traded under the name of H. W. Carter & Co and went on to see its products all over England. Foster Clark, as we have seen, would dominate the market, so that by the 1910s his bottles constituted the majority of fruit juice throwaways, rivalled only by 'The Cambridge Lemonade'. Such was his reputation by the late 1890s that he no longer needed the expensively embossed image of the Eiffel Tower on his bottles. Early ones, such as the two from Hempstead, had popularised the brand among children.

Soda water was supplied locally too. The pit contained eleven egg-shaped fizzy drinks bottles, of quarter-pint capacity, filled by 'CALEY & SON/ NORWICH'. Of the eleven, nine were embossed and two were etched, showing the different ways the firm got its name on its bottles, though, judging by the relative numbers, acid etching was either a late innovation for Caley's or a brief experiment. All dated before 1898, when Caley's became a private company, adding 'Ltd' to its name. Another bottle of this kind advertised 'STEWARD PATTESON FINCH & C⁰/ MANUFACTURERS/ NORWICH'. It dated no later than 1895, when the company registered as 'Steward & Patteson Ltd', and came from the very bottom of the cesspit. A stone bottle for ginger beer had no marks or transfer to reveal the name of the purveyor, probably because it came from a small local firm. Such firms preferred paper labels, which were cheaper than commissioned stamps or burnt-in logos. In Norwich ginger beer and soda cost a penny a bottle. The sodas may have been mixers for sherry or claret cup. The Eastern Daily Press for 31 August 1896 gave notice of a fete, the following Thursday, which the Kendalls were hosting for the church restoration fund. The rector had secured the band of the 7th Dragoon Guard along with a baronet, Sir Francis Boileau, who would open the bazaar at 3.15pm. This event or similar may have created much of the waste that ended up in the rectory cesspit.

Over the summer, Kendall tutored young men to prepare them for admission to Cambridge. He also took on a number of undergraduates, who lodged at the rectory for tutorials in the long vacation. Kendall taught them Political Economy, Political Science, and – his favourite – Constitutional History, using Stubbs' *Select Charters*.[10] In 1901, he was tutoring six students at the rectory, no doubt mindful of his children's expenses at boarding schools in Oxford.[11] He charged two guineas a week, including beer or cider but excluding wine or spirits.[12] The privy pit contained little evidence of alcohol, except for an intact wine bottle, several broken ones, a smashed decanter and glasses, and a metal hip flask for spirits (Fig. 64). The paucity of drinking refuse, also apparent at Guston, argues that drinks were fetched in jugs from a pub, and that wine bottles were re-used unlike containers for prepared fruit juice crystals and soda water. Evidence for re-use came in the form of four broken necks from wine bottles datable to the mid nineteenth century and decades-old when discarded. Though these might have been thrown away in a clear out, similar early examples from the pits at Guston and Marshbrook favour a

Figure 64. A metal hip flask (right), and two tins for scouring powder.

different interpretation, pointing to a tendency for retaining the bottles (Figs 65 and 66). Compartmentalizing their pantries, Victorian housekeepers still placed wine bottles in a category of useful vessels, with cups and jugs say, while learning to categorise other bottles as disposable packaging. Various jugs were found amid the rubbish, including a giant that contained two quarts. They served in fetching beer from the publican, and milk and cream from the dairy, a job deputed to servants. 'Purchase of milk normally implies possession of a jug or mug', wrote an observer in London, after a navvy bought a farthing's worth in 'a strong paper bag – slipped into another, slightly larger.'[13] Cream only required disposable packaging when travelling from afar. A jar from the 'WEST LONDON DAIRY COMPANY LIMITED' ended up in the Kendalls' pit, perhaps because it was too small for fetching and because its lack of a lip made it useless as a creamer. Tea, weighed and sold in bags, created no waste at the rectory. Cocoa, in contrast, may have arrived in some of the tins that lay rusting in the cess. Caley's sold it in tins that advertised the firm.

Several large bones spoke for a middle-class diet, with meaty cuts of lamb, beef, and pork. The Kendalls probably enjoyed homemade relishes as well as shop-bought ones, but the latter generated waste in the form of empty bottles. One still kept part of its label, identifying the contents as Crosse & Blackwell's Mango Chutney. A second retained its 'Stipendum Stopper', a cork bung with a malleable, composite headpiece, stamped with details of the product.[14] This

Figure 65. Fragments of early or mid nineteenth-century bottles from Marshbrook.

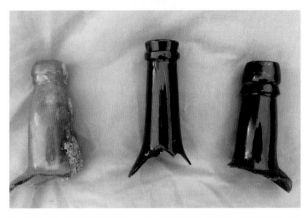

Figure 66. Necks of early or mid nineteenth-century bottles from Hempstead.

stopper, in the popular colour 'terra cotta', announced the contents: 'FRANK NEWBURY'S BOMBAY RELISH, 6^D, EXETER' (Fig. 67). Another bottle for the same condiment, although missing its stopper, could be identified from its shape as a twin brother. An empty bottle of 'LEA & PERRINS WORCESTERSHIRE SAUCE' lay in a bucket at the bottom of the pit. In a pointless but common ritual the stopper had been replaced after the contents had been emptied, presumably when the decision had already been taken to throw the useless container away. Did burying the parts separately seem like dismemberment? Although bottled sauce was not the sole preserve of the middle class, few were the occasions when the labourers at Guston would have spent sixpence on a luxury that enabled the Kendalls to enjoy spicy flavours from India. Yet the flotsam of imperial trade also jostled with

85

Figure 67. A terracotta Stipendum stopper, in the neck of a 'Bombay Relish' bottle.

refuse associated with local specialities. No gourmet can move to Norfolk and not be drawn by the seafood. Great Yarmouth was renowned for its smoked herrings, called 'bloaters', which were made into paste and potted. Legend told of how a fisherman, once, had netted an uncommonly poetic specimen:

> There was a herring spoke,
> And only one
> And that said: 'Roast my back
> Before you roast my bone.'[15]

Such was the recipe for success. Kendall purchased his bloater paste from the famous Yarmouth company, Blanchflower & Sons, whose preparations won prize medals at the international fisheries exhibitions.[16] Their prize pastes came in expensive ceramic jars with screw-on lids, four of which turned up in the privy, together with a pâté dish embossed with a lobster (Figs 68 and 69). The act of eating the pâté would have brought the lobster to light. Tasty lobster could be had from Sheringham or Cromer. Three tall tubular bottles once contained dried French olives. Such packaging seldom appears in the rubbish of the poor. A very large tin for Colman's mustard (powder) – a Norwich product – joined a number of small oval tins, which may have been Colman's 'penny ovals', though disposable tins like them were also sold containing cinnamon powder.

Figure 68 (right). Pots for Blanchflower's potted meats or fish pastes. The gap beneath the words 'HOME MADE' allowed for different labels, depending on the product.

Figure 69 (below). A continental dish for lobster pâté.

Advances in the canning and bottling industries at this time were making a range of processed foods available to a public that had more money in its pockets. Now, in addition to the fibre-depleted staples of white flour and refined sugar, the respectable family could more often indulge in spicy relishes and preserved meats. These dietary trends increased the prevalence of particular ailments associated with digestion, such as stomach troubles, constipation, and haemorrhoids. Medicinal bottles in the rubbish deposits of the late Victorian era tell the uncomfortable story. Relief for the Kendalls came from Bavaria, in the contents of a little bottle that had been packed into a crate and shipped across the North Sea. Embossed upon its base was the name of its place of origin, the spa-town CARLSBAD. Dr Jaworski, who was the expert in the matter of carbonated salts from Carlsbad, described, in his monograph, how water from the mineral springs was evaporated, filtered, cooled, and caused to crystallize. In 1878–9, a municipal building had been erected there for the preparation of the salt. After that, the improved Carlsbad salt had been developed, 'a white, finely crystalline powder, which is sent out into commerce in cylindrical bottles under the name of *Natürliches Karlsbader Sprudelsalz (pulver form)*'.[17] As the advert from the 1890s makes plain, any product not sold in a cylindrical bottle, labelled with the Carlsbad seal, in a blue carton, was not genuine (Figs 70 and 71). The rival Kutnow's Powder, whatever else it contained, could hardly pretend to contain *Karlsbader Sprudelsalz*. Kendall had the genuine product to hand.

Dr Jaworski conducted a number of experiments on presumably willing subjects to monitor the effect of this product on the bowels. Subject no. 18 was a 26-year-old clergyman, suffering severe constipation. Jaworski noted, in this case, that passages were generally produced by injections of water into the rectum. Two days passed without a stool emerging, before Jaworski administered 5 grams of Sprudel Salt in 250 cubic centilitres of water at 18°C, two hours after supper. The dose was repeated in half an hour. During the night, the constipated cleric experienced rumblings in the abdomen, and his sleep was disturbed. Not until morning, after twelve hours, did he produce 'a mushy stool'. In a second experiment, comparable to the first, the patient complained of 'a great distension of the stomach, followed after three hours by a copious watery stool, accompanied by the passage of much *flatus* (*i.e.* wind)'.[18] Perhaps he preferred the enema he knew. After examining 40 cases, Dr Jaworski concluded that Carlsbad Sprudel Salt expedited the movement of the bowels. There was nothing mushy about the science underpinning the Kendalls' choice of remedies. Indian chutneys, French olives, and bloater paste from Yarmouth all exited with a proven German laxative.

Figure 70 (above). An advert for Sprudel Salts, showing the bottle with label etc. 1898.

Figure 71 (right). The Sprudel Salts bottle from Hempstead, with CARLSBAD embossed upon its base. c. 1895.

Most of the medicine bottles in the pit were unembossed phials or obloid 'flats', probably from local chemists, who favoured labels over the more costly embossing. Occasionally these chemists did pay for the latter, and one specimen bore the name 'COUSINS & THOMAS, OXFORD', where the firm traded at 20 Magdalen Street. Another, made at the same glassworks, had come from the same chemists no doubt. Bottles from chemists in Oxford did not often find their way to rubbish pits near the Norfolk coast, but in this instance the bottles may have travelled when the Kendalls moved from the Cotswolds. A second example, embossed 'RICHARDS & Cᵒ', had been produced in a plate mould, in which a metal plate engraved with one company's name could be removed and replaced with another, so that any number of differently embossed bottles could be made in the same mould. Favoured by local chemists, the plate mould made embossing affordable by obviating the need to make a new mould for each retailer. Apart from more than a dozen unembossed bottles, of the varieties used for cough mixture, magnesia, and the like, three bottles displayed the details of proprietary remedies, namely Elliman's Universal Embrocation, Allen and Hanbury's Castor Oil (in cobalt glass), and Chesebrough's (original) Vaseline. In the 1890s, as the evidence shows, local chemists accounted for the bulk of medicinal preparations. Twenty years later, as the last refuse pit in Guston revealed, chain-store pharmacists were taking their custom. Judging by the number of bottles, we should conclude that the Kendalls spent more on medicine than the poorer folk in Guston and Marshbrook. Respectable medicines were expensive; they contained expensive ingredients, which had to be prepared and mixed. The bottles scarcely lent themselves to re-use. Richer folk acquired more of them and threw more away.

Among the household items were the usual glass preserves jars, including broken patent specimens by the Kilner brothers, London, and the London glassworks Breffits Ltd, which used an early bottle-making machine. Three or four ceramic jars made by the potters Maling of Newcastle had been thrown away intact. Maling had contracts with several firms, including the marmalade makers Keiller and Sons of Dundee, to supply jars for marmalade and jam. Another ceramic jar might have contained mock turtle soup or tobacco. Hexagonal blue poison bottles resembled the bottles found at Guston and Marshbrook, but vessels for glue or paste revealed that the Kendalls had no need to make adhesives at home, following recipes given in books such as *Facts and Hints*, which advised that 'common glue' must always be at hand.[19] A tiny bottle embossed 'T. O. & COˢ MEND ALL Regᵈ' had contained patent cement. Seven white ceramic glue pots may have been involved in decorating when the Kendalls moved in.

Figure 72. Enormous master inks, with pouring lips, made at the Doulton pottery in Lambeth, c. 1895.

Other stoneware included a large bottle for blacking, a small one for a similar product, three for furniture cream – joined by three squat cylindrical glass vessels for the same substance with 'STE[PHENSON BROTHERS] FURNITURE CREAM' surviving on the label – and eight master inks of various sizes in cream and brown stoneware, with pouring lips. Two were truly gigantic, holding a quart each (Fig. 72). These ones and a smaller one were stamped with the mark of the Doulton pottery, Lambeth. Another was manufactured by Bourne of Denby. The presence of only one inkwell-bottle was further evidence that the Kendalls, unlike the labourers at Guston, had inkwells. As a highly literate household, involved in tutoring, they poured their ink voraciously and threw away the bottles. Kendall had penned many essays. He once wrote to his tutor at King's complaining about a Mr Hammond, who had given him 32 for his Political Philosophy paper: 'the best paper I have sent in for years... He said he couldn't read it: but that doesn't trouble me: I have it from him now and it is admittedly plain if not beautiful. But I don't mind: he doesn't examine in the Tripos'.[20] In the Tripos, which he took that summer, Kendall obtained a First. He later became Professor of History at Queen's College, London, after writing a short history of the Anglican Church.

The large number of stoneware bottles – I counted 26 (20 intact) excluding jars for jam, *etc.* – is partly a testament to the costs of manufacture, still relatively low in the 1890s, and partly a consequence of consumption patterns within that household, which tended towards several products sold in ceramic containers, notably ink, glue, and expensive fish paste for spreading on sandwiches at the rectory. Without all the master inks, glue pots, potted meats, and furniture cream bottles, the refuse dumped by the labourers at Guston, *c.* 1900, contained far less stoneware. Sundry luxuries at Hempstead included glass paraffin lamps and the remains of a large ceramic boiler, 'THE GOURMET BOILER, CHALLIS PATENT, No. 12'. A child-sized bone toothbrush spoke of the children's dental hygiene. Even the cast-iron lid of a patent sanitary paper holder and the soap dish from the privy ended up in the pit (Fig. 73), along with a few mould-blown jars that must have been sitting around for years; a pair of transfer-printed plates, with a hunting theme, showing a dog and a deer; the rector's metal hip-flask; pieces of his shotgun (!), bricks, rubble, tiles, and smashed window glass, with bits of lead flashing.

Figure 73. Metal and ceramic sanitary buckets. The items in the foreground are a soap dish (right) and the metal lid of the sanitary paper holder, with the royal coat of arms.

Figure 74. A fragment of the patterned lino used to seal the pit.

There were so many broken oil lamp flues that a clear out seems likely. One was embossed 'FIREPROOF', another, 'HINKS', naming the lamp makers Hinks and Son, of Birmingham and London. Flues of this sort were machine moulded. Once the pit was filling up and the sloping shaft under the toilet hole was nearly full, Kendall or his servant laid a cut of old linoleum over the in-fill at the bottom of the latter, beneath the box-like structure of the toilet seat, which must have been dismantled by that point. The lino is printed with a geometric Arts and Crafts design, of the 1870s or 1880s, and was probably from a leftover cut sitting around in an outbuilding (Figs 74 and 75). Bricks were then stacked on the lino and wedged into the shaft, until it was filled to a point level with the floor. Perhaps the privy seat was then put back, with a bucket underneath. It was about the turn of the century that many people in East Anglia were filling in these pits and installing hygienic buckets, which were emptied at regular intervals. Alternatively, they may have used the privy as a potting shed, laying the flowerbed over the rubbish for the gardening rector to sow his seeds. Some of his throwaways are captured in Figures 76, 77, and 78.

Figure 75. The cesspit almost empty. The shaft to the right slopes upwards towards the place where the wooden seat once stood, inside the privy building.

Figure 76. Bottles and jars from the privy, c. 1895. Top row, left to right: chutney or pickle jars, wine, chutney, magnesia, feeding bottle (?), chutney jar, mango chutney, honey, Caley's mineral water. Second row, left to right: five lamp flues, two bottles for dried olives or similar, furniture cream, ink, Lea & Perrins Worcester Sauce, ink, mineral waters (×4). Third row, left to right: three medicine bottles, two bottles for Bombay Relish, two bottles for perfume or toiletries, medicine phial, condiment (?), ink, two bottles for dried olives, medicine, specimen vase, two paraffin lamps. Bottom row, left to right: ten bottles for De Carle's fruit syrups, ink bottle, three small bottles for furniture cream, assorted small bottles (×5).

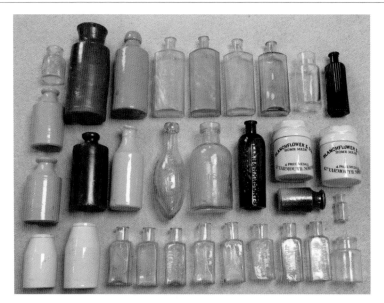

Figure 77. More bottles and jars from the privy. Top row, left to right: Chesebrough's Vaseline, blacking, ginger beer, Cousins & Thomas of Oxford, three more medicine bottles, Sprudel Salts, poison. Middle row, left to right: two furniture creams, one on top of the other, two inks with pouring lips, Caley's mineral water, Mellin's Infant Food, Allen & Hanbury's Castor oil, two Blanchflower's pots over a furniture polish bottle and a tiny adhesive 'Mend-all'. Bottom row, left to right: two paste/ glue pots, eight bottles for fruit juice crystals from De Carle's of Nowich, Foster Clark's, and Gill's of Bristol, a jar for pills or powder.

We can compare the Kendalls' rubbish to the waste generated by another literate and relatively prosperous household, namely the school house at Bergh Apton, south east of Norwich. In 1896 the schoolmistress was Miss Anna B. Horrex, aged 27, and she ran the school with her widowed mother Maria, who taught needlework, and her sister Edith, who took the infants. They enjoyed the use of the school house rent free, and their combined salaries amounted to £112, with Anna earning £84 p/a, Edith £16 p/a, and Maria £12 p/a. The school house they lived in was joined to the western end of the school, which the children would have entered by the front door before taking their seats at the three rows of desks that faced the stove and, behind it, their point of entry. Each row was three desks deep, one row being occupied by the first class, one by the second class, and the third by 'children'. The teacher's

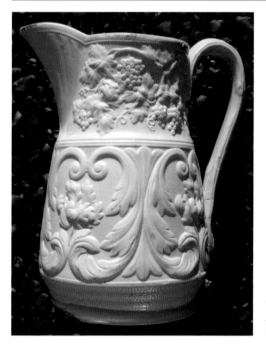

Figure 78. A wine jug from the privy. Cleaned and repaired by Dr Tim Pestell.

desk was positioned to be closer to the last two sets, at the front on the right hand side as one entered. There was a smaller room to the rear for infants, separated from the classroom by a curtain. Average attendance in 1896 was reported as 51, but surviving log books show that it varied. Across the lane was the churchyard, bounded by a wall, adjacent to a disused gravel pit. Night soil was carted and deposited here beyond the hedge. The surviving school logs record that in the 1880s and '90s, the landowner Mr Norman was paid to send men to clear out the school cisterns (*i.e.* the latrines). In January 1884, the sum owing was 4 shillings and sixpence; by October 1889, it had risen to 5 shillings. The cesspit served as a convenient tip for the Horrexes. Members of Bergh Apton history group found a scattering of rubbish from the late 1890s strewn on top of the clay cap that had been laid down to seal Mr Norman's night soil pit.[21]

Among this refuse were items linked to the activities of the school itself, such as the glass and metal inkwell, ink bottles, slates, and the slate pencil that can be seen in Figure 80. The slates have lines on one side, for writing on, and squares on the other, for sums. Entries in the school log bring them to life. In

Figure 79. In his later years Kendall was a canon of Norwich Cathedral. Here he is (the short figure in the centre) outside the west front on Wednesday 13 August 1930. Reproduced by kind permission of the Dean and Chapter of Norwich Cathedral.

June 1883, for example, Edward Everett was caned 'for cleaning his slate directly the master ordered him not to do so'. He had been scribbling inappropriate messages to a classmate. In March 1885, Albert Bracey was cautioned about playing with the ink stand – possibly the very one shown in Figure 80, which is of the right date. The external casing of wood or leather has rotted away. There were also fragments of a mid-Victorian nursery rhyme cup that came from the Staffordshire potteries. The sepia transfer shows a seated man next to the head of a large mouse, on one side, and a builder with his tools on the other, flanking a rhyming couplet (with the missing bits restored below in italics):

I WAS AN ITAL*IAN*
WHO HAD A WH*ITE* MOUSE

J WAS A JO*IN*ER
WHO BUILT U*P* A HOUSE

The rhymes are from 'Tom Thumb's Alphabet', which was a popular aid to learning throughout the nineteenth century. Originally, this cup would have been one of a set of thirteen, each illustrating two letters of the alphabet.

Figure 80. Three ink bottles with burst-off lips (left); glass and metal inkwell (centre), and slates, with part of a slate pencil (top right). 1890s.

Past schoolmasters including William Plumpton in the 1880s and James Walker in the early 1890s had lived there with children of their own, so the mug may either have been for the schoolchildren or for a child of one of the teachers (Fig. 81). Another item connected with the Victorian school was a ceramic Spode pen case, decorated with strawberries, and dated after 1852 by its diamond registration mark. It turned up in the midst of rubbish from the school dumped in the late 1940s, encrusted with grime and a contents of fused rusty nails as though it had been relegated to a shed many years before it was eventually discarded.

Other rubbish revealed the throwaway habits of the Horrex schoolmistresses. A number of chemists' bottles bore the names of family firms in Norwich. Ubiquitous proprietary medicines were present as well, including Elliman's Embrocation, Eno's Fruit Salts, and Beetham's Glycerine and Cucumber for beautifying the skin. Potted meat went down well in the Horrex household, with several pots, whole and broken, surfacing in the trench. George Plumtree's pot (Fig. 82) dates from after 1895, when his factory was still located at 164 Portland Street. The plain pot was perhaps from a smaller local company that made its own products, applying paper labels. Cracroft's toothpaste pot, in

Figure 81 (above). Pearl ware cup, with a sepia transfer illustrating I and J from 'Tom Thumb's Alphabet'. Made in Staffordshire.

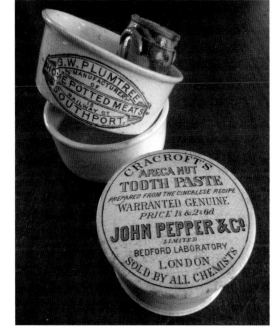

Figure 82 (right). Cracroft's Areca Nut Toothpaste (lid and pot); plain potted meat or fish paste pot; Plumtree's potted meat pot, from 13 Railway Street, Southport (after 1895); and a mustard barrel. 1890s.

Figure 83. Ivory, bone, and horn objects, discarded in London and dumped in Essex. Top left: gaming counters and a cane handle, carved as a fist holding a snake. Top centre: dominoes (left one retaining its ebony base) and the bottom of a chess piece. Below: babies' teething rings. Right and bottom left: toothbrushes. Bottom centre: part of a cutthroat razor. The shell-like object above is a carved mute for a cello or double bass. Bottom right, mouthpieces for tobacco pipes. 1880s–90s.

contrast, advertises the firm's products not only on the top but also on the underside of the lid, where there is an advert for Sulpholine soap. At a shilling a pot it was a luxurious purchase in expensive disposable packaging. The blue barrel appears to be a promotional mustard pot, possibly from Colman's of Norwich. Such throwaways were matched by the quality of the crockery, which included a few decorative wares. Here, as at Hempstead, literacy and wealth generated its own distinct categories of waste. Other throwaways from a range of Victorian dumps can be seen in Figures 83–89.

Figure 84. Children's bits. These may have been swept up and discarded accidentally before making the journey, with the London dust, out to the Essex marshes. Top left corner: dolls' cups, plates, lids, and a pot. Centre: pieces for the game Five Stones in various colours. Bottom left: marbles. Right, top to bottom: bone counter; tiny dolls called Frozen Charlottes; glass dolls' eyes; lead horse; bisque mouse; bone counter. 1880s–90s.

Figure 85. Casualties of the nursery. Bisque and china dolls, discarded in London and dumped in Essex. Can you spot the pug? 1880s–90s.

Figure 86. Buttons, beads, and other small items, made of bone, glass, milk glass, jet, and mother of pearl. The large glass object in the centre is a sugar crusher, broken at one end. Many of these items would have been attached to clothing when discarded. 1880s–90s.

Figure 87. More casualties. Lead soldiers from rubbish dumps, 1890s–1910s. Note the puttees worn by the headless Scottish infantry.

Figure 88. Penknives and pocket watches. The item top right is a stamp box. Found in rubbish dumps.

Figure 89. Work and play. The flat iron is from a tip outside Canterbury, c. 1905. The leather cricket ball was discarded in London and preserved in the mud of the Essex marshes. 1890s.

Notes

1. S. Strasser, *Waste and Want: a Social History of Trash* (New York, 1999), p. 9.
2. *Kelly's Directory for Norfolk, 1896*, p. 167.
3. Godfrey, no. 231, by Baker and Co Ltd, England.
4. Mellin's Food Company, *Diet after Weaning: a Manual for the Care and Feeding of Children between the Ages of One and Two Years* (Boston, Massachusetts, 1907), pp. 9, 10.
5. Bell, *At the Works*, p. 211.
6. Godfrey, nos 1732, 958, 2713, 231, 263, 1332 (Doulton, US Patent 314002).
7. G. R. Sims, 'London's Light Refreshments', in *Living London*, ed. G. R. Sims, 3 vols (London, 1902–3), III, pp. 49–56, at p. 49.
8. *Armstrong's Norfolk Diary: Further Passages from the Diary of Benjamin John Arnold*, ed. H. B. J. Armstrong (London, 1963), p. 185.
9. *Victorian Party-Giving on Every Scale*, first printed as *Party-Giving on Every Scale* (1880), reprinted (Stroud, 2007), pp. 51–2, 55, 36, 47, 57, 44, 48, 38, 114–16.
10. King's College, Cambridge. OB/1/900/A: Letter, 6 June 1903, to Oscar Browning.
11. King's College, Cambridge. OB/1/900/A: Letter, 28 September 1901, to Oscar Browning.
12. King's College, Cambridge. OB/1/900/A: Letter, 4 October 1901, to Oscar Browning.
13. P. F. William Ryan, 'Scenes from shop and store London', in *Living London*, ed. Clarke, III, pp. 140–6, at p. 144.
14. See the advert reproduced in Edward Fletcher, *Collecting Pot Lids* (London, 1975), p. 21.
15. Ernest R. Suffling, *The Land of the Broads*, 7th edition (Stratford, 1895), p. 105.
16. See the advert reproduced in Colin Tooke, *The Great Yarmouth Herring Industry* (Stroud, 2006), p. 124.
17. Dr W. Jaworski, *The Action, Therapeutic Value and Use of the Carlsbad Sprudel Salt (Powder Form) and its Relation to the Carlsbad Thermal Water*, translated from the German by A. L. A. Toboldt (Philadelphia, 1891), pp. 9–10.
18. *Ibid.*, p. 18.
19. *Facts and Hints*, p. 214.
20. King's College, Cambridge. OB/1/900/A: Letter of 7 April 1887, to Oscar Browning.
21. Norfolk Record Office, PD 497/36 is the School Managers' Minute Book, and MF 1496/4, contains the school log from 1883 to 1901.

⇜ Conclusions ⇝

STROLLING through Whitechapel in 1903, Mr William Ryan found a recycling shop, stocking rags and bones, waste paper, old furniture, bedsteads, 'mysterious little heaps of battered metal, bottles, and time-worn books'.[1] For more than thirty years London had buried its rubbish unsorted or consigned it to the flames of the destructor, yet here was a mini-economy in recycling, in one of the poorer parts of the city. A year earlier, in 1902, the same gentleman had noted that scavengers still picked through dust heaps in certain districts, and that the zinc bins in the streets were scavenged for anything of value – which meant pretty much anything – a messy job, given that the contents were 90% ash.[2] What separated the scavengers from the members of a throwaway society was their attitude to the remaining 10%. There was always a spectrum of attitudes, as one shaded into another, and notions of what was disposable shifted, but by and large the trend across the period covered by this book, 1875–1914, was that more people in town and countryside joined the society of waste-makers. We can be very precise too about the increase in waste, which came not in excess coal dust, rags, or paper, but in packaging made of glass and metal, often intended to be used once then thrown away. There is a difference between disposing of an item because it is broken and throwing away an item because it is empty. Only in the period we have examined did the latter become conventional (Fig. 90).

Karl Marx, had he written on this subject, might have regarded it as the ultimate form of alienation, by which the fruit of one person's labour – namely, a hand-made bottle – was enjoyed neither by its maker nor by the customer, who would discard it as soon as possible. Only at the very end of this period were the majority of jars and bottles being made in machines, which eliminated the need to dispose of hand-made objects, not because the practice was deplored but in the interest of labour reduction. Nor would Marx have objected necessarily, because packaged products were labour saving: they improved the condition of the workers, and especially their wives, who no longer had to prepare so many household substances, now that prepared varieties were sold cheaply. The drive towards machine production, complete by 1918, drove down prices, allowing

Figure 90. A trench into an early twentieth-century dump in a disused sand pit reveals a typical layering, mostly of ash, breeze, and cinders, interspersed with crockery. This was the result of numerous rounds of the village dust-cart. In 1914, ash and burnt coal from domestic fires still constituted up to 90% of dry refuse.

the masses to join the market. It was over this period the vast majority learned that, though they had always known that bottles and jars should be kept, some should be thrown away. In the 1870s, as we saw at Guston in the case of the round-bottomed soda and thin-necked sauce bottle, this applied only to the most impractical. By the 1910s there were so many bottles and jars that supply had vastly outstripped the demands of re-use. Even where people kept a few, they threw a load away. Solid, black-glass wine bottles of former decades were regarded as part of the pantry furniture, to be thrown away only when broken. Versatile stoneware jars and bottles belonged to the same category, but monofunctional vessels for ink, medicine, or lemonade crystals were thought of, and designed, as disposable packaging. It was the firms behind the products they contained who introduced waste, where none had previously arisen. Railways and steamships, and new possibilities in far-flung trade, added to the flow, when products had to be bottled, packaged, and canned for travel.

It is remarkable how much the Kendalls' rubbish spoke of overseas trade, with ceramics from China, Japan, and Limoges, Mango chutney, Bombay relish, French olives, and Bohemian health-salts; but we should not overlook the German mineral water and remedies and Belgian preserves jars in the refuse at Marshbrook; nor for that matter the Argentine beef that went into the labourers' Bovril at Guston, or the Indian tea, harvested from the plantations in Ceylon and bottled by Lipton's. Many vessels had travelled before ending up in the ground, when Devonshire cream, sold fresh in London, was finally eaten in Kent; or when Beach's bottled fruit was taken far from its factory and consumed in Shropshire; or when Foster Clark's fruit juices journeyed from Kent to Hempstead (probably via a Norwich caterer named Pike) to refresh the rector's children on a summer's day. Even so, most of the rector's drink, food, and medicine, would have been supplied locally. This was true, in fact, of his fruit juice crystals (mostly made by De Carle's of Norwich), his fizzy drinks (Caley and others), his beer and cider (locally produced no doubt), his milk and cream, his medicines, with occasional exceptions, and probably his meat. Only when the great brands had gained wide recognition and started to move their produce around more did labourers in Kent and postmen in Shropshire enjoy familiar branded sauces and Boots' products; bottled tea from Ceylon; Bovril, Brasso, and the rest. These firms could pay for marketing and package and deliver products cheaply. By 1915, waste was beginning to display generic qualities as local variation gave way to an orderly array of brands. Stoneware had already given way to glass; and hand-finished glass had largely given way to machine-made vessels. Despite the flux, stoneware bottles were kept for brewing, and things lingered in cupboard corners. The stuff from one generation never goes away completely with the incoming tide of the next.

Humans in all generations are equal, in that we consume and waste. Nor is any one of us (except for a privileged few) exempt from mundane chores. The desire to obtain greater command of our time and resources by reducing the amounts of each we spend on preparing food and other necessaries impels us, in the absence of more pressing considerations, to invest in ready-made products as the means to achieving this end. The custody of objects – the cleaning, repairing, and storing of bottles, for example – also makes demands on us that we would rather avoid. We always have that motive to respond favourably to packaging that invites us to throw it away. For by throwing it away, we rid ourselves of a tedious obligation. In the era 1875–1914 our throwaway society was established, reliant on the rise of products in disposable packaging. Despite interludes of austerity and re-use during the two World Wars, it has, as a general trend, grown ever more assertive in affirming our wasteful identity. After learning to discard hand-made ones of stoneware and glass, it took to wasting machine-made vessels and an increasing number of cans, before making the switch, during the second half of the twentieth century, to throwing away plastic packaging along with glassware, metal, paper, and card. Then the throwaway society began to dispose of white goods and electronics. Whereas in 1900, waste from London went mostly into Essex and Kent, to be scavenged by local children, by the year 2000, e-waste from London was ending up in India, where children pick through the refuse, searching for valuable metals and components and creating toxic fumes by burning away plastics. The throwaway society has always been adaptable, even resourceful. But to dwell on its evolution is to distract from its source.

Today we discard packaging our grandparents would never have imagined. To save ourselves the labour of the most trifling tasks, we purchase washed ready-made salad and ready-grated cheese in plastic bags that go into our dustbins. We head over to the supermarkets for sliced vegetables packed in plastic trays, in plastic wrapping, or purchase a tiny quantity of fruit salad in a lidded plastic container from the snack counter, helping ourselves to disposable plastic cutlery which is wrapped up in clear plastic. Muffins are sold in muffin-shaped plastic containers, as takeaway snacks. If we want water we buy it in plastic bottles, though many of the drinks we buy in such vessels contain addictive sugars which prompt us to consume and discard more than we need. We consume far more than our grandparents, and for different reasons. Far more of our eating and drinking is for pleasure, and we throw away more waste food.

Although we recycle more packaging than our grandparents, we re-use less, which is unfortunate, because recycling consumes more resources than re-use. It is an inferior solution to waste. The best solution to waste is not to waste; and there is no evidence that we do so instinctively. Before mass production introduced disposable packaging, containers were kept and repaired. Even in a consumer age there are small things we can all do to help our society reverse some of its throwaway habits. For instance, we can drink more tap water instead of bottled drinks. We can buy unwrapped fruit and vegetables and bread. If possible, we can purchase local produce rather than the sort that has to be packed and conveyed long distances. A few little habits like these may counteract the temptation to waste more and more for our convenience. Maybe then the rubbish we leave for our grandchildren will speak of our concern for their world, should they ever dig it up to tell our story.

Notes

1. Ryan, 'Scenes from shop and store London', p. 144–5.
2. P. F. William Ryan, 'London's toilet', in *Living London*, ed. Sims, II, pp. 196–201, at p. 200.

Further Reading

Cessford, Craig, 'Assemblage biography and the life course: an archaeologically materialized temporality of Richard and Sarah Hopkins', *International Journal of Historical Archaeology* 18 (2014), 555–90.

Fletcher, Edward, *Bottle Collecting* (London, 1972).

Gandy, Matthew, *Recycling and the Politics of Urban Waste* (London, 1994).

Jeffries, Nigel, 'The Metropolis Local Management Act and the archaeology of sanitary reform in the London Borough of Lambeth 1856–86', *Post-Medieval Archaeology* 40 (2006), 272–90.

Lucas, Gavin, 'Disposability and dispossession in the twentieth century', *Journal of Material Culture* 7: 1 (2002), 5–22.

Owens, Alastair; Jeffries, Nigel; Wehner, Karen; Featherby, Rupert, 'Fragments of the modern city: material culture and the rhythms of everyday life in Victorian London', *Journal of Victorian Culture* 15: 2 (2010), 212–25.

Packard, Vance, *The Waste Makers* (London, 1961).

Strasser, Susan, *Waste and Want: a Social History of Trash* (New York, 1999).

Turvey, Ralph, 'Economic growth and domestic refuse in London', in Sasson, H., and Diamond, D., ed., *LSE on Social Science* (London, 1996), pp. 217–35.

White, Carolyn L., ed., *The Materiality of Individuality: Archaeological Studies of Individual Lives* (New York, 2009).

Places to Visit

The Museum of Brands, Packaging and Advertising
(Mr Robert Opie's collection)
2 Colville Mews, Lonsdale Road,
Notting Hill, London, W11 2AR

The National Bottle Museum
Elsecar Heritage Centre,
Barnsley, South Yorkshire, S74 8HJ

The History of Advertising Trust Archive
12 Raveningham Centre,
Raveningham, Norwich, NR14 6NU